**National Soccer Coach** **Association of America**

COACHING COURSE MENU

Intermediate

- Level 3
- Level 4
- Level 5
- Level 6
- Special Topics

Advanced

- National Diploma
- Advanced National Diploma
- Premier Diploma
- Master Coach Diploma

Beginner

- Level 1
- Level 2

Goalkeeping

- Level 1
- Level 2
- Level 3
- Advanced National

High School

Intermediate Level Courses

- NFHS Fundamentals of Coaching
- High School Diploma

Director of Coaching

Intermediate Level Courses

- Director of Coaching
- Member Club
- Club Standards

COMPLETE SOCCER COACHING CURRICULUM FOR 3-18 YEAR OLD PLAYERS - VOLUME 1

EDITED BY

David Newbery - eLearning Coordinator, NSCAA

ACTIVITY CONTRIBUTIONS BY

David Newbery - eLearning Coordinator, NSCAA (Stage 1 – 3-5 year old players)

Sari Rose - Assistant Technical Director of Coaching and Player Development, North Carolina Youth Soccer (Stage 2 – 6-8 year old players)

Ian Barker - Director of Coaching Education, NSCAA, (Stage 3 – 9-11 year old players)

Robert Parr - Director of Coaching, Arkansas State Soccer Association, (Stage 4 – 12-14 year old players)

Tony Englund - Author of FC Barcelona - Style and Domination, (Stage 5 – 15-18 year old players)

FRONT COVER DESIGN AND LAYOUT

Kathleen Hermesch - Graphic Designer, NSCAA

PROOF READING

Valerie Brown - An excellent mother in-law!

ACTIVITY ILLUSTRATIONS

Artlife Design and Illustration

PRODUCED BY

Coaching Media Group   NSCAA eLearning

DAVID NEWBERY, EDITOR AND AUTHOR OF STAGE 1
eLearning Coordinator, NSCAA

Since 1988, David has studied and worked in youth education, soccer development and coaching. A former University Professor and CEO of a Youth Sports Company, David has been fortunate to travel extensively in the USA, meeting with coaches and club officials and learning about their approach to player development and coaching. David oversees the NSCAA eLearning program and is Coordinator for NSCAA Club Standards Project. David developed the 5 Stage of Development Pathway used as a framework for this manual in 2007 (an adaptation of the LTAD model from Canada). He contributes articles regularly to soccer publications, has written books focusing on player and coach development and presents at national soccer events. In a volunteer capacity David operates a youth soccer program for player's age 3 to 11 in Connecticut and Rhode Island.

SARI ROSE, AUTHOR OF STAGE 2
Assistant Technical Director for Coaching and Player Development, North Carolina Youth Soccer

Sari works full time in youth development and coach education. Soccer has been a significant part of Sari's life and has been involved as a player, coach and administrator. Rose had a stellar career at Wake Forest where she studied for bachelors degree in politics and religion. As a four-year varsity letter winner Sari was the starting goalkeeper for the first ever Wake Forest women's soccer team. Sari spent 7 years as an NCAA Division I College Assistant Coach and Recruiting Coordinator, taught English and social studies for two years at High School and traveled with the US State Department to Bahrain, Saudi Arabia, Qatar and Palestine to promote youth sports. Amongst her numerous qualifications, Sari has achieved NSCAA Advanced Diploma, NSCAA Regional Goalkeeping, USSF National Youth License and USSF B License. Sari is the Youth Girls Representative on the NSCAA Board of Directors.

IAN BARKER, AUTHOR STAGE 3
Director of Coaching Education, NSCAA

Ian has held leadership positions with US Youth Soccer and NSCAA and he has had extensive experience at youth and college levels. Ian coached for 21 seasons with the men's programs at the University of Wisconsin and Macalester College, before becoming NSCAA Director of Coaching Education in 2012. Ian was the Director of Coaching and Player Development for Minnesota Youth Soccer Association for 10 years and is a Head Coach of Region II Boys Olympic Development Program. Ian has extensive international coaching experience, including: New Zealand, Brazil, Italy, Uganda, Spain, Argentina, Costa Rica and Germany. Ian's qualifications are extensive and he holds the USSF 'A' License, NSCAA Premier Diploma and NSCAA Master Coach Diploma. Ian graduated from University of Warwick with a Bachelors Degree in Philosophy and Literature and a Post Graduate Certificate of Education in English.

ROBERT PARR, AUTHOR OF STAGE 4
Director of Coaching for the Arkansas State Soccer Association and NSCAA Club Standards Project Consultant

Robert Parr has spent 27 years in the game as a coach and program director at both the youth and adult levels. He holds a USSF A license, NSCAA Premier Diploma, and a USSF National Youth Coaching license. Previously, he served as the Director of Coaching and WPSL Head Coach for the Puerto Rico Capitals FC, the first international franchise to compete in the Women's Premier Soccer League. From 2003-2008, he was the Head Women's Soccer Coach at Georgia College & State University and also coached for the Georgia State Soccer Association Olympic Development Program. Previously, Robert was the Director of Training for the American Soccer Club "Eagles", South Texas Men's State Team Coach and a South Texas YSA State Staff Coach for both the Olympic Development Program and the Coaching Education Program. He is the co-creator of SoccerROM.com and he has helped author or edit 3 soccer-related books.

TONY ENGLUND, AUTHOR OF STAGE 5
Assistant Director of Coaching at Sporting St. Croix Soccer Club and Academy

Tony has over twenty four years of high-level coaching experience. For over a decade, Tony has worked is a Director of Coaching capacity and is the Assistant Director of Coaching at Sporting St. Croix Soccer Club and Academy. Tony is the High School Boys Coach for Mahtomedi High School, leading then to the State Championship quarter finals in 2014. Tony has been An NSCAA Associate Staff Coach since 2001 and holds more has a dozen NSCAA coaching awards. He has a masters degree in diplomatic and military history from the University of Minnesota. He is a frequent presenter at symposiums and clinics in the Midwest, he is also the author of four popular soccer coaching books, including 'Style and Domination: A Tactical Analysis of FC Barcelona' that is sold in over 30 countries. Tony's most recent book is 'The Art of the Duel - Elite 1vs1 Training, focuses on a most critical aspect of the modern game, the importance of winning an 'battle 1v1 over an opponent.

NSCAA EDUCATION PARTNER PROSPECTUS

National Soccer Coaches Association of America invites youth soccer clubs in North America and around the globe to become an **NSCAA Education Partner.**

NSCAA offers a club with an opportunity to provide its coaches, administrators, parents and players with access to free and low cost education content that is flexible and responsive to the needs of its members. NSCAA eLearning provides a club with clinics and courses delivered live and/or on-demand that will supplement and existing training program or establish a clear in-house education framework.

Features:

1. Coach access to dozens of free presentations and downloads, including introductions to Attacking and Defending Principles of Play.
2. Free access to NSCAA Level 1 Diploma - a free, on-demand online course for beginner and intermediate coaches, release date April 1, 2015.
3. 'Partner Pricing' on all current and future eLearning presentation and clinics, including NSCAA Player Development Curriculum: a 5 Stages of Player Development training program for coaches working with 3-18 year old players.
4. Use of the NSCAA brand and logo on the organization's website as an Official **NSCAA Education Partner**.
5. Access to tracking and reporting on the education performance and attainment of the organization's members*.
6. Free introductory 6 month Membership to NSCAA for all new individual members*.
7. Free enrolment as an NSCAA Member Club. Benefits include: discount on individual full membership, registration for NSCAA Convention, tournament advertising and much more.*

Note: *Tier 2 and 3 NSCAA Education Partner benefits

Partnership Levels:

Tier 1 (free)

+ The NSCAA Education Partner promotes NSCAA eLearning to its members.
+ Posts the **NSCAA Education Partner** logo prominently on the home page of the organizations website with a link to NSCAA eLearning.
+ NSCAA refers to the organization as an 'Official **NSCAA Education Partner**' and post the organization's logo on NSCAA.com.

Tier 2 ($1000)

+ A Tier 2 **NSCAA Education Partner** receives all Tier 1 benefits, plus:
+ A unique education URL (i.e. nscaa.adobeconnect.com/name_of_club)
+ NSCAA will create with the club, a 2-3 minute club introductory presentation to proceed the course content. Content to include, welcome, club philosophies, club mission, style of play presentation, etc.
+ Special NSCAA eLearning promotions, such as deep discounted pricing, exclusive screening of new content and early registration for programs with limited registration.

To learn more and register to be an NSCAA Education Partner, visit www.NSCAA.com/eLearning
or contact David Newbery at dnewbery@nscaa.com or 401-377-7008.
Features, benefits and pricing correct as of December 1, 2014 and are subject to change.

EDUCATION. WHERE YOU WANT IT.
WHEN YOU WANT IT. HOW YOU WANT IT.

National Soccer Coaches Association of America

NSCAA AFFILIATE EDUCATION PARTNER PROSPECTUS

National Soccer Coaches Association of America invites associations, corporations, league organizers and other stakeholders in coaching education and player development to partner with NSCAA. As an NSCAA Affiliate Education Partner, your organization will receive full support to achieve the objective of providing convenient and affordable high-quality learning experiences to your membership. By incorporating NSCAA's significant on-demand content library with your organization's current education initiatives, collaboratively we can offer richer and more convenient educational experiences for your members and greatly reduce operating costs. In fact, this partnership opportunity can also generate a revenue stream to help financially support your education plans.

Features:

1. Provide your members with dozens of free presentations and downloads.
2. Partner Pricing' on all current and future eLearning presentation and clinics, including NSCAA Player Development Curriculum – potentially free education giveaways to your members.
3. Co-branded presentations.
4. Collaborate with NSCAA to create new eLearning content utilizing NSCAA eLearning delivery platform.*
5. Affiliate Education Partner's own education unique URL.*
6. Set up live training events with virtual classrooms, video conferencing and rich-media content.*
7. Access to tracking and reporting on the education performance and attainment of the organization's members.*
8. Corporate NSCAA Member.*

Note: *Tier 2 and 3 NSCAA Education Partner benefits

Partnership Levels:

Tier 1 (free)
+ NSCAA Affiliate partner promotes NSCAA eLearning to its members.
+ Posts the **NSCAA Affiliate Education Partner** logo prominently on the home page of the organizations website with a link to NSCAA eLearning.
+ NSCAA refers to the organization as an 'Official **NSCAA Affiliate Education Partner**' and post the organization's logo on NSCAA.com.

Tier 2 ($1500)
+ A Tier 2 NSCAA Affiliate Education Partner receives all Tier 1 benefits
+ A unique education URL (i.e. nscaa.adobeconnect.com/name_of_organization)
+ NSCAA will create with the organization, a 2-3 minute club introductory presentation to proceed the course content. Content to include, welcome, philosophies, etc.
+ All member clubs introduced by **NSCAA Affiliate Education Partner** will be connected to NSCAA content via the affiliate's URL and will receive affiliates messaging.
+ Special NSCAA eLearning promotions, such as deep discounted pricing, exclusive screening of new content and early registration for programs with limited registration.

Tier 3 (free)
+ A Tier 3 **NSCAA Affiliate Education Partner** receives all Tier 1 and 2 benefits.
+ 5% of all club spend on eLearning products once the affiliate has introduced 10 or more Tier 2 clubs (see NSCAA Education Partner Prospectus on previous page.

To learn more and register to be an NSCAA Affiliate Education Partner, visit www.NSCAA.com/eLearning or contact David Newbery at dnewbery@nscaa.com or 401-377-7008.
Features, benefits and pricing correct as of December 1, 2014 and are subject to change.

EDUCATION. WHERE YOU WANT IT.
WHEN YOU WANT IT. HOW YOU WANT IT.

VOLUME 1 - **TABLE OF CONTENTS**

Dear Coach,

On behalf of the National Soccer Coaches Association of America, we would like to thank you for purchasing this **'Complete Soccer Coaching Curriculum for 3-18 year old Players'**. Packed with 100 coaching activities, curriculum diagrams and an abundance of coaching tips, our approach to player development is constructed around a 5 Stage Model. This manual focuses on all 5 Stages, 3-18 year old players and is an excellent resource for an experienced and novice coach alike.

The manual supports NSCAA Player Development Curriculum Diploma Course Season 1, an eLearning program offered by National Soccer Coaches Association of America. To learn more about NSCAA eLearning, visit www.NSCAA.com/eLearning. NSCAA is committed to delivering coaching education in a variety of methods – methods that reflect different learning styles and interest levels of our members. Presenting vibrant and engaging content in a convenient and low cost elearning format to supplement and enhance existing NSCAA courses and events is a priority.

It is now possible for a coach, at their convenience, to participate in highly informative and tremendously interesting courses and presentations and receive formal recognition/credit for participation. Benefits of eLearning are considerable, both for the individual and NSCAA. Expect to see many more low cost opportunities in the near future to engage with top professional educators without the need to leave your home, office or local library.

There are 4 manuals now available to support NSCAA Player Development Curriculum Diploma Course Season 1:

1. **Soccer Coaching Curriculum for 3-8 year old Players – Volume 1**: with activity contributions from David Newbery, eLearning Coordinator, NSCAA and Sari Rose, Assistant Technical Director of Coaching and Player Development, North Carolina Youth Soccer.

2. **Soccer Coaching Curriculum for 6-11 year old Players – Volume 1**: with activity contributions from Sari Rose, Assistant Technical Director of Coaching and Player Development, North Carolina Youth Soccer and Ian Barker, Director of Coaching Education, NSCAA.

3. **Soccer Coaching Curriculum for 12-18 year old Players – Volume 1**: with activity contributions from Robert Parr, Director of Coaching, Arkansas State Soccer Association and Tony Englund, Author of FC Barcelona - Style and Domination.

4. **Complete Soccer Coaching Curriculum for 3-18 year old Players – Volume 1**: includes all 5 stages of development in one manual.

We hope you enjoy the manual. Please don't hesitate to provide us with feedback relating to the webinars, manual and discussions.

Kind Regards,

David Newbery and Ian Barker

David Newbery
eLearning Coordinator, NSCAA
dnewbery@nscaa.com

Ian Barker
Director of Coaching Education, NSCAA
ibarker@nscaa.com

INTRODUCTION - **CURRICULUM DESIGN**

The term 'Curriculum' is most commonly associated with teaching and school education. In general terms, an educational curriculum consists of everything that promotes intellectual, personal, social and physical development of the participants. When transferred to sport, the term curriculum is usually related to a book of activities and games organized in such a way to aid the coach plan for a practice session. Rarely do these curriculum books engage the reader in a rationale for selecting such activities, or describe how coaching methodology is as important as the activities themselves. Unfortunately this approach usually leads to very low adherence by the coaches – particularly if subsequent coaching sessions do not realize the outcomes suggested in the text.

In the context of youth soccer, learning is often left to chance. Clubs and coaches seem satisfied to accept the major benefits of participation as activity and having fun. Although these outcomes are very beneficial to the child, wider ranging results can also be realized through a structured and organized program – a 'true' curriculum. Soccer participation offers children experiences to develop confidence, self esteem, knowledge, physical development and in some cases the opportunity to participate in elite level competition at High School and College.

The NSCAA Player Development Curriculum details the framework, aims, objectives and content that creates tremendous value and helps to raise standards, performance and expectations. The curriculum includes approaches to teaching, learning and assessment, quality of relationships between coach and the player and the values embodied by the club.

NSCAA APPROACH TO CURRICULUM DESIGN

In partnership with practitioners and curriculum experts, NSCAA has developed an approach to curriculum design based upon three key elements:

1. Element 1: Curriculum Aims
2. Element 2: Curriculum Organization
3. Element 3: Curriculum Evaluation

ELEMENT 1 **WHAT ARE WE TRYING TO ACHIEVE?**

The NSCAA Player Development Curriculum provides an opportunity to create a relevant, coherent and engaging environment for all players, parents and coaches. Having clear purposes representing the club's hopes and desires for the players is an important starting point. Purposes not only provide a reference point for decision making but also a direction on how learning experiences are to be organized.

Curriculum Purposes

The purposes of the NSCAA Player Development Curriculum are:

1. Establish an entitlement – for every child entering the program irrespective of social background, wealth, gender or differences in ability.
2. Establishes standards – at each stage of development so progress of players and coaches can be monitored, goals and improvement targets can be established and players can be selected for the appropriate development groups.
3. Promotes continuity and coherence – facilitates the transition of players between teams and phases of skill development, and provides a framework for coaches to adhere to.
4. Promotes understanding for parents and players – increases understanding and confidence in the player development philosophy and coaching team.

Curriculum Aims

The NSCAA Player Development Curriculum aims to:

1. Provide attainment standards for measuring coach and player performance
2. Reflect best practice
3. Promote intellectual, social, personal and physical development
4. Establish high expectations for all constituents
5. Identifies outcomes relating to skills, knowledge and other performance criteria
6. Reflects the vision and mission of NSCAA
7. Provide equal opportunity for all players to learn and achieve

Curriculum Outcomes

A successfully implemented NSCAA Player Development Curriculum will result in:

1. Players enjoying playing and learning
2. Players committing to playing and learning
3. Result in best possible progress
4. Achieve highest attainment for all players
5. Develop player and coach confidence
6. Offer opportunities to work individually and as a team
7. Enable players to think creatively and critically and solve problems

ELEMENT 2 HOW DO WE ORGANIZE LEARNING?

The NSCAA Player Development Curriculum is developed from the work of Istvan Bayli. Now widely adopted in many sports in Canada and Europe, the Long Term Athlete Development System was adapted by David Newbery to become relevant to soccer and in particular, recreation and travel soccer programs. Commencing with the youngest players, the curriculum is organized into building blocks of learning – learning that is deep. When appropriately implemented, the building blocks will stack together to form a pathway of teaching and learning experiences appropriate for all players.

There are several components that contribute to curriculum organization including: 1) Content – games and activities chosen to accomplish a coaching outcome; 2) Methodology – a wide variety of approaches to teaching and instruction to encourage player participation and learning; 3) Supporting knowledge – scientific evidence, philosophies and opinions underpinning the curriculum model; 4) Learning Environment – consideration of the different types of soccer provision and interaction between practice and competitive play.

By understanding the dynamic interplay between these four factors, NSCAA can help every player make progress, building on their experiences both at club organized training and competitions, at home or at the park with friends and family. To this end, one objective of the curriculum is to encourage players and parents to appreciate that learning experiences should occur beyond the scheduled club activities. In fact, in many countries around the world, players develop their knowledge and understanding more quickly by watching high level play on TV or in person at live games and by dedicating 'homework' time to individual ball mastery.

Considering the critical relationship between coaching and curriculum, the curriculum document and games and activities must not be used in isolation. It is imperative that coaches firstly understand about the players (stage of development, level of proficiency, interest and commitment etc). Secondly, they choose the activities wisely to meet the needs of the player, team and environment and thirdly they adopt measures to continually assess progress of players and coaches.

ELEMENT 3 HOW WELL ARE WE ACHIEVING OUR AIMS?

The concepts of assessment and evaluation regularly cause concern and are uncomfortable topics. This is no truer than in a youth sports environment where assessment is typically associated with selection. In soccer, assessment means tryouts and tryouts are designed to answer one question – are you good enough to play travel soccer?

Assessment has it place, it should be used at every opportunity to make a difference for learning. Assessment should also be fit for purpose – the quantitative and qualitative methods used must be appropriate to the stage of development and also relevant to the skill, knowledge or behavior being tested. Identifying the appropriate level of play for a particular child often provides an organization with a number of sensitivity issues. Talent identification should not be restricted to a once a year occurrence, but needs to be an ongoing process involving coaches, players and parents. Ultimately, the aim of a talent identification program is to ensure that all players have the opportunity to progress at a rate and level that their talent and development allows. Matching the resources and expertise to meet the needs of the player requires both an internal and external perspective.

A progressive assessment process encourages a variety of methods. For example, utilizing several assessors to evaluate players can offer strength to the process, as does the use of video analysis.

PURPOSE, AIMS AND OUTCOMES

1. What is the purpose of the curriculum?	**Aims**	Equality of Opportunity	Establishing standards	Continuity and coherence	Promotes understanding	Pathway (3-18+ year old players)
	Outcomes	Achieve soccer standards	Achieve academic, social and health aims	Commitment to learning	Confident learners	Individual and team success
	Focus		Skill development (individual and team)	Knowledge and understanding (e.g. identifying visual cues and tactical awareness)	Attitudes and attributes (e.g. sportsmanship, respect, and confidence)	
2. How is the curriculum structured?	**Content**	Fundamental movement skills	Tactical awareness and understanding	Physical and mental preparation	Academic and social responsibility	Fundamental soccer skills
	Methodology	Practical and theory	Individual and team assessment	Guided practice	Self-discovery	Directed and modeling
	Supporting knowledge	Cognitive development and mental acumen	Biological development, growth and maturation	Emotional development, confidence and self-esteem	Nutrition, balanced diet and hydration	Physical fitness, speed, agility, balance and coordination
	Learning environment	Team practices, positional instruction and optimal sessions	Street soccer and unstructured practice	Competition (e.g. 11 v 11 and small-sided games)	Tournaments and festivals	Indoor training and games
3. Are the aims being achieved?	**Evaluation**	Skill acquisition (Against performance standards)	Team selections (Tryout process combined with regular seasonal assessments)	Talent identification (Planning for exceptional talent)	Knowledge and understanding (Decision-making and tactical awareness)	360 Review (Parents, players, coaches, and administrators)

THEORY OF PLAYER DEVELOPMENT

The NSCAA approach emphasizes development-appropriate skill acquisition to maximize the player's potential. The supporting theory supports ever more complex and demanding conditions placed on the player as they advance through several stages of development, which include pre-puberty, puberty, post-puberty and maturation. In addition to physical transformations, the model also accounts for changes in emotional and cognitive development, factors having a dramatic effect on the capacity of players to learn and perform. Significant developmental differences also exist between children of the same gender and same age. To this end NSCAA model supports the adage – "if you are good enough ... you are old enough". It is extremely important to offer programming flexibility to enable each child to find their training and performance level. This perspective should not only apply to 'playing-up', but also to placing players 'down'. Our focus must always be on what is best for the child – a decision involving a number of variables. One reason players plateau and leave soccer is an overemphasis on competition instead of training during the important period in their athletic development. Stage 1, 2 and 3 are the most important phases of preparation, physically, mentally, emotionally and in the development of key soccer skills of dribbling, passing and control.

PLAYER DEVELOPMENT PATHWAY

Children entering soccer at aged 3, 4, 5 or 6 will start a 'journey' that should have a clearly defined beginning, middle and end, including multiple assessment points and learning experiences. Some players and parents will choose to end the journey early, but for others who aspire to play soccer into adulthood, the Player Development Model manages every step of the way. For many players and parents understanding the steps to success, expected outcomes and focus on education and training are extremely important factors. True Player Development provides such a pathway, building programs around principles that respect the developmental needs of all children.

STAGES OF DEVELOPMENT

Originally a model for Elite Athlete Development, the NSCAA pathway provides a process for development from early childhood through retirement. Stage 1 (4 and 5 year olds), Stage 2 (6-8), Stage 3 (9-11), Stage 4 (12-14) and Stage 5 (15-18). Each stage of the model promotes a different development focus – the interplay between physical, cognitive, emotional, psychological and social variables. For example, when working with four and five year olds consider that players of this age tire easily, need repetition and reinforcement, have short attention span and mostly approach tasks individually.

In terms of soccer participation, we need to ensure the sessions are short, activities change constantly, skills are demonstrated and continually reinforced and information needs to be camouflaged and concealed, such as using cartoon characters and creating a story for a particular activity. Importantly, every child should have a ball at their feet for the vast majority of time. Team play at this stage of development should be restricted to small sided games and 1v1 situations. As players move into Stage 2 we start introducing passing and working cooperatively with teammates.

LEARNING FOCUS

In the context of youth soccer, learning is often left to chance. Clubs and coaches often seem satisfied to accept the major benefits of participation as activity and having fun. Although these outcomes are very beneficial to the child, wider ranging results can also be realized through a structured and organized program. Regardless of age and ability a Player Development Coach is focused on nurturing players to achieve end of stage goals and attainment targets.

To this end, NSCAA has developed a Player Development Competency Matrix (4-18 years old). Benchmarks for performance are provided at the end of each stage of development. The assessment program measures the players 'competence' – the relationship between skill, selection and application of skills, tactics, strategies and ideas and the readiness of body and mind to cope with the activity.

Stage of Development	Stage 1			Stage 2			Stage 3			Stage 4			Stage 5			
Age in years	3	4	5	6	7	8	9	10	11	12	13	14	15	16	17	18

PHYSICAL LITERACY SKILLS

	3	4	5	6	7	8	9	10	11	12	13	14	15	16	17	18
Run with stops and starts	−			+												
Run and change directions	−			+												
Gallop	−			+												
Skip	−			+												
Lateral movements - side-step	−			+												
Rolling, bending low, arching	−			+												
Balance - on a line	−			+												
Balance - on one foot	−			+												
Throw - strong hand	−				+											
Throw - weak hand	−				+											
Jump - make shapes in air	−		+													
Jump - one foot to another	−		+													
Jump - stride and bound patterns	−						+									
Jump - hurdles	−						+									
Quick feet and crossovers		−			+											
Speed - Coordination of arms and legs					−					+						
Speed - explosive first step						−				+						
Running technique		−								+						
Sprinting technique						−				+						

DRIBBLING SKILLS

	3	4	5	6	7	8	9	10	11	12	13	14	15	16	17	18
Turns - basic	−				+											
Turns - advanced				−			+									
Dribbling basics	−				+											

Competency based coaching: this approach suggests performance improvements are acquired progressively – meaning, competency in basic skills/knowledge must be achieved before progressing to more complex skills and concepts. With this in mind, the Competency Matrix helps coaches to know when players should be 'Introduced' (−) to a skill/concept and when players should be expected to demonstrate 'Competency' (+).

Stage of Development	Stage 1			Stage 2			Stage 3			Stage 4			Stage 5			
Age in years	3	4	5	6	7	8	9	10	11	12	13	14	15	16	17	18
DRIBBLING SKILLS CONTINUED																
Running with the ball				-			+									
Feints and dribble		-						+								
Beating an opponent			-					+								
Escaping an opponent			-					+								
RECEIVING																
Control - Foot			-							+						
Control - Thigh					-						+					
Control - Chest						-						+				
Control - Head						-						+				
PASSING																
Ground - Inside of foot - 5 yards				-				+								
Ground - Inside of foot - 10 yards					-				+							
Ground - Inside of foot - 20 yards						-					+					
Ground - Instep						-				+						
Long pass						-						+				
Chip/Lofted pass							-					+				
Swerve pass - inside of foot							-					+				
Swerve pass - outside of foot							-					+				
Crossing							-					+				
SHOOTING																
Instep			-						+							
Half volley						-					+					
Volley						-					+					

Competency based coaching: this approach suggests performance improvements are acquired progressively – meaning, competency in basic skills/knowledge must be achieved before progressing to more complex skills and concepts. With this in mind, the Competency Matrix helps coaches to know when players should be 'Introduced' (-) to a skill/concept and when players should be expected to demonstrate 'Competency' (+).

COMPETENCY MATRIX

Stage of Development	Stage 1			Stage 2			Stage 3			Stage 4			Stage 5			
Age in years	3	4	5	6	7	8	9	10	11	12	13	14	15	16	17	18
SHOOTING CONTINUED																
One on one with Goal Keeper								-					+			
HEADING																
Basic technique				-							+					
Defensive header							-						+			
Attacking header							-						+			
PHYSICAL CONDITIONING																
Own body weight strength exercises								-								+
Core body strength								-								+
Dynamic warm-up						-										+
Flexibility							-									+
Aerobic Endurance training									-							+
Anaerobic Endurance training									-							+
Speed training (Anaerobic)									-							+
MENTAL/COGNITIVE CONDITIONING																
Confidence	-												+			
Commitment							-									+
Concentration	-												+			
Composure							-									+
GOAL KEEPING																
Basic Catching Techniques						-				+						
Positioning							-				+					
Diving								-					+			
Distribution								-					+			

Competency based coaching: this approach suggests performance improvements are acquired progressively – meaning, competency in basic skills/knowledge must be achieved before progressing to more complex skills and concepts. With this in mind, the Competency Matrix helps coaches to know when players should be 'Introduced' (-) to a skill/concept and when players should be expected to demonstrate 'Competency' (+).

Stage of Development	Stage 1			Stage 2			Stage 3			Stage 4			Stage 5			
Age in years	3	4	5	6	7	8	9	10	11	12	13	14	15	16	17	18

GOAL KEEPING CONTINUED

	3	4	5	6	7	8	9	10	11	12	13	14	15	16	17	18
Advanced Techniques - crosses, punching etc										-						+

SET PLAYS

	3	4	5	6	7	8	9	10	11	12	13	14	15	16	17	18
Throw in				-				+								
Penalties				-						+						
Corners				-								+				
Goal Kicks				-						+						
Free Kicks				-										+		

ATTACKING PRINCIPLES AND TECHNIQUES

	3	4	5	6	7	8	9	10	11	12	13	14	15	16	17	18
Attacking as an individual 1v1		-										+				
Attacking in pairs (2v1 and 2v2)				-								+				
Attacking in small groups (3's and 4's)							-							+		
Attacking as a unit and team								-								+
Support with and without the ball						-							+			
Attacking from wide positions								-						+		
Crossing balls into the penalty box								-						+		
Transition and counter attacks							-									+
Finishing						-										+
Attacking set plays									-							+
Communication							-									+
Positional Play						-										+

DEFENSIVE PRINCIPLES AND TECHNIQUES

	3	4	5	6	7	8	9	10	11	12	13	14	15	16	17	18
Defending as an individual 1v1 - pressure				-						+						
Defending in pairs (2v1 and 2v2) - pressure and cover						-						+				

Competency based coaching: this approach suggests performance improvements are acquired progressively – meaning, competency in basic skills/knowledge must be achieved before progressing to more complex skills and concepts. With this in mind, the Competency Matrix helps coaches to know when players should be 'Introduced' (-) to a skill/concept and when players should be expected to demonstrate 'Competency' (+).

Stage of Development	Stage 1			Stage 2			Stage 3			Stage 4			Stage 5			
Age in years	3	4	5	6	7	8	9	10	11	12	13	14	15	16	17	18

DEFENSIVE PRINCIPLES AND TECHNIQUES CONTINUED

	3	4	5	6	7	8	9	10	11	12	13	14	15	16	17	18
Defending in small groups (3's and 4's) - pressure, cover, balance									-					+		
Defending as a unit and team										-						+
Marking								-					+			
Recovery							-					+				
Communication							-							+		
Transition from defense to attack							-									+
Defensive set plays								-					+			
Positional Play							-									+

LAWS OF THE GAME

	3	4	5	6	7	8	9	10	11	12	13	14	15	16	17	18
Individual and Team Behavior	-									+						
Field and Equipment		-								+						
Restarts				-			+									
Fair and foul play	-									+						
Basic Rules	-					+										
Free kicks - offside, direct and indirect etc				-						+						
Misc laws - advantage etc					-					+						

Competency based coaching: this approach suggests performance improvements are acquired progressively – meaning, competency in basic skills/knowledge must be achieved before progressing to more complex skills and concepts. With this in mind, the Competency Matrix helps coaches to know when players should be 'Introduced' (-) to a skill/concept and when players should be expected to demonstrate 'Competency' (+).

LONG TERM FOCUS

Research exists suggesting that becoming an Elite athlete requires dedication of 10,000 hours. Three hours of practice every day for 10 years. Although this elite level of performance outcome is only applicable to a very small percentage of the playing population, this example does illustrate a correlation between time, maturation and achievement. The NSCAA Model represents a more realistic perspective of commitment, focusing more on the quality of instruction, ratio of practices to competitive games and self dedicated time, than on the volume of hours. However, becoming a competent performer takes time as the body and mind need to adapt to growth and experience. Unfortunately, in youth soccer a short term perspective is regularly implemented by coaches and parents with an over-emphasis on winning and achieving immediate success – this has been referred to as 'Peaking by Friday' mentality.

Progression is a term used frequently in soccer coaching to represent advancement in training complexity or applying coaching conditions to increase demands on the players. Progression is also used to describe how coaches gradually build learning experiences in stages rather than all at once, coordinating the instruction and content with the player's motivation and developmental phase. In moving too quickly to tactics, formations and positions, coaches will pass over general movement skills and gradual skill progression. This is a significant oversight as failure to become proficient in the fundamentals of the game and in movement will create deficiencies in performance later. For players and parents with aspirations of playing soccer in college or beyond, failure to master the foundations of the game will affect their opportunities in adult sport.

HOLISTIC APPROACH TO LEARNING

Former USA Women's National Team Coach, Tony DiCicco uses a phrase 'Soccer sessions life lessons' to describe the role soccer should play in developing characteristics such as leadership, team work, commitment and responsibility. Participation in sport and physical activity not only helps to shape character traits but can also contribute to better academic performance.

A strongly held belief by many administrators of town soccer is the perception that fun and learning are mutually exclusive – if we make the environment more conducive to learning (small side activities, ability based, player assessments, individual instruction, shorter and more focused sessions etc) we sacrifice fun. This belief has no scientific foundation and in fact flies in the face of common logic. In cases where programs cite bad experiences in implementing a 'learning environment', we propose the issue is more in the way implementation was approached and communicated, than in the idea itself. In his book 'Good to Great', Jim Collins addresses organizations having an issue in changing when their current approach is seemingly realizing good results. Collins refers to 'good being the enemy of great' and this is certainly applicable to youth soccer. Why change the approach to learning when participation numbers in soccer exceed all other sports in the town?

We must also think of ways to encourage players to learn the sport outside of scheduled practices and games. Taking the ball out in the yard with friends and parents, attending a live game (high school, college or professional) or watching the game on TV are some of the ways we can further engage players and parents in the learning experience. Finally, NSCAA believes a Player Development Model should encourage players to play a variety of sports for as long as possible, until such times as the player decides to commit more fully to soccer. Soccer performance can benefit significantly by learning from physical transfers from other sports and vice versa. For example, tactical similarities such as attack and defense in basketball or field hockey - rebounding, quick feet and lateral movements in basketball can greatly enhance explosive movements required in soccer. Playing soccer 3-5 nights per week for a 7 year old child is too much. We do however recommended players participate year round to limit performance regression – developing their competencies in movement and fundamental ball skills.

THE PLAYER DEVELOPMENT CONTINUUM

Stage 1	Stage 2	Stage 3	Stage 4	Stage 5
3 to 5 years	6 to 8 years	9 to 11 years	12 to 14 years	15 to 18 years

CONTINUUM OF PLAYER DEVELOPMENT

Player Development Continuum: Development occurs on a continuum where development is more important than the chronological age of the player. Developmental differences between players of the same age are common place and can correlate to +/- 2 years of chronological age. Thus, in a mixed ability group of 10 year old players, it is feasible to have players performing at a level of an average 8 year old and an average 12 year old - a 4 year development range.

5 STAGES OF DEVELOPMENT MODEL

Age in years	0-3	4	5	6	7	8	9	10	11	12	13	14	15	16	17	18
Bayli LTAD	Active start			Fundamentals			Learning to train			Training to train				Training to compete		
Stage of Development	Stage 1			Stage 2			Stage 3			Stage 4				Stage 5		
Age groups	U4-U6			U7-U9			U10-U12			U13-U15				U16-U19		
Soccer age (development)	2 years +/-			2 years +/-			2 years +/-			2 years +/-				2 years +/-		
Coaching time per year	40-90 hours			100-120 hours			150-320 hours			150-320 hours				150-540 hours		
Developmental focus	Social			Technical			Technical			Technical				Tactical		
	Physical			Social			Social			Tactical				Psychological		
	Technical			Physical			Tactical			Physical				Technical		
	Psychological			Tactical			Physical			Psychological				Physical		
	Tactical			Psychological			Psychological			Social				Social		
Specialist training	No positions			Attack and defend			Specialist positions			Groups and units				Whole team		
Players per session	12			12 to 15			12 to 18			12 to 18				18 to 22		
Length of session	30 to 45 mins			45 to 60 mins			60 to 90 mins			75 to 90 mins				75 to 90 mins		
Training to game ratio	Training only			4:1			3:1			3:1				2:1		
Training format	1v1 to 3v3			1v1 to 5v5			1v1 to 8v8			4v4 to 11v11				4v4 to 11v11		
Game format	Training only			3v3 to 5v5			5v5 to 8v8			7v7 to 11v11				11v11		
Player assessment frequency	Once per season			2 per year			3-4 per year			3-4 per year				4+ per year		
Coach certification	NSCAA L1-3			NSCAA L1-3			NSCAA L3-6			NSCAA National				NSCAA National +		

GROWTH AND DEVELOPMENT

Physical and emotional changes that occur as people mature affect all aspects of life, including sport. A child centered coach needs to understand the different phases of development and how they can affect sports performance – particularly coaches of young athletes. Coaches need to consider not only the player's physical needs but also their social, emotional and cognitive needs. Adapting teaching methodology and content to meet the player's needs significantly improve their progress in soccer. Training, competition, and recovery programs should be designed to match the physical, mental, cognitive, and emotional development of each player. Ethics, fair play and character building should also be taught according to each child's ability to understand these concepts at different ages.

Discussions about development center around two factors - Growth and Maturation: 'Growth' refers to measurable changes such as height, weight and fat percentage. 'Maturation' refers to more subtle qualitative adaptations, such as cartilage changing to bone. Noticeable and subtle changes in growth and maturation are referred to as development, and these include social, emotional, intellectual, and motor performance. There is also a distinction between chronological age (days and years since birth) and development age (the degree of physical, mental, cognitive, and emotional maturity). The development age of the player is of primary importance to the successful implementation of the NSCAA Player Development Curriculum. As a player's developmental age can differ by as much as two years from their chronological age, it is important that all content and teaching methodologies are appropriate to development. For example, a player who is 12 calendar years old could be 10 to 14 in developmental age.

Knowing if a player is an early, average, or late developer is critically important in adopting an approach to coaching. This knowledge will provide the basis for determining the starting point and capacity of a player to absorb information and perform. Most importantly, appreciating where a player is situated along the Player Development Continuum allows for the coach to plan for individual needs. Failure to recognize development cues can contribute to several negative outcomes, including selecting teams based on size, strength and speed. Research has concluded that children born in the first third of the year (i.e. January to April for sports using the calendar year) have a statistically significant advantage over children born near the end of the year. However, research also concludes that children with late birthdays eventually draw alongside their older peers and in many cases surpass performance levels. Unfortunately, many average and late developers do not reach their full soccer potential when they are passed-over at age 10, 11 or 12 and don't receive good coaching, patience and perseverance.

The development considerations for each stage in the curriculum are explored in the 'Stage' sections of this curriculum.

CHILD CENTERED CURRICULUM

Central to the theme of Player Development is the concept of 'Child-centered' learning. The focus of the NSCAA Player Development Curriculum is the need of individual players (child) – first and foremost. The education environment is constructed to focus on the player's, abilities, interests, and learning styles and the coach performs as the facilitator. At each stage of development the player should actively participate in creating learning experiences. Individual performance outcomes should largely direct coaching content and activities. Conversely, 'Coach-centered' approaches have the coach as the central director and players in a passive, receptive role.

A 'Child-Centered Coach' uses a variety of techniques to engage the players in thought and discussion. One technique used consistently is questioning. Questions give children an opportunity to solve a problem and typically players try hard to solve it. Solutions generated to address the issues are theirs and subsequently players take greater ownership than if they were told what to do, when to do it and how to do it. Solving problems through questioning enables players to explore, discover, create and generally experiment with a variety of techniques and tactical processes.

There are several approaches to help players reflect on their learning while practicing and playing games:

+ Skill questions develop purposeful feedback and skill awareness. Skill questions include what and where. For example, What happened to the ball when you lean back? Where did your head finish when you took that shot?
+ Tactical questions develop decision making and problem solving with respect to the strategies of the game/activity. Tactical questions include how and why. For example, how can you and your teammate work together to get into a position to score a goal? Why did you run faster this time?
+ Review questions develop thinking skills to help modify activities to make it more challenging, enjoyable and inclusive. For example, what did you enjoy about this activity? What would you change about this activity? What did you learn about this activity?

FUNDAMENTAL MOVEMENT SKILLS (FMS)

As soccer coaches, we spend a considerable amount of time and energy planning sessions to develop fundamental soccer skills. This is particularly the case with the youngest players entering soccer for the first time at age 4, 5 or 6. However, whether consciously or unconsciously, we all too often overlook the foundation for fundamental soccer skills – fundamental movement skills.

Naturally we should expect parents, preschool and school systems to provide young players with instruction and exposure to skills such as walking, running, jumping, skipping, kicking, catching and throwing. Unfortunately, evidence suggests many children do not receive suitable movement education and as a result they stay at the elementary stage of skill development. Failure to acquire movement skills by the end of Stage 2 (8 years) has a dramatic effect on the progress potential for children in youth sports programs. In a wider context, children need to develop basic physical skills and a degree of competence to continually participate in physical activity, not just sport. Perceptions about physical activity formed during the first few years of participation provide the key to future motivation and participation. In general, movement skill acquisition leads to confidence and performance successes that in turn lead to continuous adherence to a sport or physical activity.

As previously discussed, before progressing on to more complex skills, it is imperative the child can competently perform foundation and basic skills. Fundamental movement skills are the building blocks upon which all sport skills are based and must be mastered before learning more complex, specialized skills like those needed in games, sports and recreational activities. To this end, movement competence is a prerequisite for fundamental soccer skills. That is not to say, however, a soccer ball cannot be introduced into movement skill activities.

Fundamental Movement Skills are the building blocks upon which all sport skills are based and must be mastered before learning more complex, specialized skills like those needed in games, sports and recreational activities.

LOCOMOTOR SKILLS	STABILITY SKILLS	MANIPULATIVE SKILLS
Involve the body moving in any direction from one point to another	Involve the body balancing either in one place (static) or while in motion (dynamic).	Involve handling and controlling objects with the hand, the foot or an implement (stick, bat or racket)
Crawling Running Galloping Walking Hopping Skipping Dodging Jumping Sliding Leaping	Stopping Bending Twisting Landing Climbing Balancing Turning	Throwing Catching Striking Bouncing Dribbling Kicking

The introduction to soccer stage coincides with the onset of independence from parents and increased self confidence in most children. Children also start to begin to play cooperatively with others. This does not mean however parents should fully pass the responsibility for learning to the club coach. The parent has a very important role in encouraging the child to play at home. Practice sessions should occur once or twice per week and players should be encouraged to play multiple sports and activities.

DEVELOPMENT FOCUS

+ Players should learn the fundamental movement skills of running (forwards, backwards and sideways), jumping, turning, twisting and bending (lowering center of gravity to form a solid base).
+ The ball should be involved all the time.

KEY DEVELOPMENT POINTS FOR CHILDREN IN STAGE 1		
Physically	**Psychological/Social**	**Cognitive/Mental**
1. Tires easily and recovers quickly.	1. Likes to play/work on their own, egocentric.	1. Increasingly able to use visual instructions (play them out of their mind), although observing demonstrations is more concrete.
2. Learns best by being physically active.	2. Easily motivated.	
3. Needs to repeat activities that are well known and mastered.	3. Enjoys initiating activities.	2. Beginning to take into account ideas and emotions of others.
4. Mainly uses large muscle movement, fine motor skills developing, but more difficult to master.	4. Enjoys being praised for endeavors. Sensitive to criticism and does not enjoy failure.	3. Inconsistent attention span.
5. Basic motor skill developing, needs to combine skills in simple games.	5. Developmentally advanced players start to become more independent and attempt to exercise more control over own environment.	4. Moving from being adventurous to be cautious.
6. Boys and girls have equal ability.		5. Interests can be short and quick changing.
7. Center of gravity is higher, resulting in issues with balance.	6. Limited attention span, 15-20 minutes.	6. Imaginative, spontaneous and creative.
	7. Frustration can come quickly.	
	8. Has a strong desire for affection and attention from adults.	
	9. Seeks social approval.	
	10. Experimental, exploratory behavior is part of development.	

DEVELOPMENT CHARACTERISTICS TRANSLATED TO COACHING PLAYERS IN STAGE 1

Child centered coaching requires a commitment on behalf of the coach/adult to embrace a natural starting point in development for each player. The coaches role is not to create parity (all players the same), but to nurture them to a level consistent with their individual commitment, attitude, enthusiasm and talent. To ensure participation in soccer is enjoyable for players, adults, parents and coaches of 4 and 5 year olds need to embrace and work with the development characteristics, and not against them.

TRANSLATED TO PLAYER DEVELOPMENT THIS MEANS

1. Significant emphasis on fundamental movement skills – running, jumping, skipping, throwing etc
2. Focusing on ball familiarization and dribbling skills – one ball per child.
3. Sessions that are simple, fun, have variety and use large muscle.
4. Selecting activities that do not place undue stress on the muscles, bones and energy systems of the body.
5. Repeating activities regularly – constant change and insufficient reinforcement negatively affects learning.
6. Including activities that take a short time to complete (5-10 minutes), due to short attention span.
7. Camouflaging and concealing technical information by using names, characters and stories.
8. Encouraging trial and error, keeping instruction to a minimum.
9. Using equipment and props to increase complexity but continue to make the sessions fun – hurdles, hoops, ladders, bean bags, etc.
10. Include competitive games, but emphasize successes other than just winning (i.e. effort).
11. Providing considerable encouragement.
12. Keep instruction to a minimum and activity regular.
13. Include 'games and matches' in every session – no need for a separate day for games.
14. Avoiding temptations to place players in specialist positions (i.e. full back, forward or goal keeper).
15. Continually reinforce effort and constantly praise players.

SPIDERS WEB

STAGES COVERED BY ACTIVITY
Stages 1, 2 & 3 - 3-11 year old players

THEMES & COMPETENCIES
Theme:
+ 1v1 attacking and defending
+ Dribbling
+ Ball mastery.

Competencies:
+ Turns and feints- basic
+ Dribbling basics
+ Fundamental movement skills
+ Beating and escaping an opponent
+ Attacking as an individual
+ Confidence and concentration
+ Defending as an individual.

WHY USE IT
Spider's Web introduces young players to the concept of dribbling to space within a confined area. As more players join the 'web', less open space is available – an excellent teaching moment for the coach to discuss head up, looking for space and changing direction to avoid pressure.

SET UP
20 x 20 yard square. 9 players each have a ball and can dribble anywhere within the square. 3 players start the web by linking arms and the 'web' can move anywhere in the square as long as arms are linked together.

HOW TO PLAY
Story: The players are on safari in the dangerous Amazon jungle. Huge spiders have made a massive web and are hoping to capture all the players. On the command of 'GO', the web starts to move around the jungle (square). If any part of the web touches the player's ball, the player must join the web and kick their ball out of the area. The game continues until all the players are caught in the web.

COACHING NOTES
+ Coaching objectives – players dribbling with the laces and 'raise their heads' to see where space exists.
+ Coaching tip – Set a touch-target. My goal for Stage 1 is 10 touches per minute per player - 300 touches in 30 minutes
+ Adaptations – make the game a direction activity, by adding a safety zone at each end of the jungle.

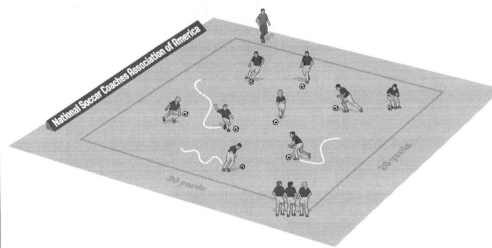

+ 3 players link arms to start the spiders web.
+ Remaining players dribble a ball in the jungle.

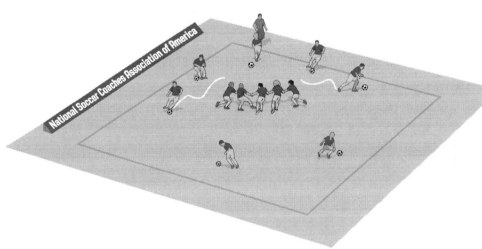

+ The spider's web grows in size if a ball is touched.
+ Players must dribble into space.
+ Players in web must keep arms linked.

+ Add 2 safety zones to make the game more 'directional'.
+ Play becomes more predictable.

PIT STOP

STAGES COVERED BY ACTIVITY
Stages 1, 2 & 3 - 3-11 year old players

THEMES & COMPETENCIES
Theme:
+ 1v1 attacking and defending
+ Dribbling
+ Ball mastery.

Competencies:
+ Turns - basic
+ Dribbling basics
+ Feints and dribble
+ Beating an opponent (2nd stage)
+ Attacking as an individual
+ Confidence and concentration
+ Defending as an individual.

WHY USE IT
'Pit Stop' is an excellent activity to activate the interest and focus of young players quickly. Consistent with the 'individual' focus at the first stage, we can differentiate the difficulty of the activity.

SET UP
20 x 20 yard square. Randomly place 6 cone gates (Pit Lane) - 2 yards apart. All players have a ball and can dribble anywhere within the square. Coach can add a number of conditions to the activity to change the emphasis, such as changing the pace of the dribble, changing direction and dribbling to space.

HOW TO PLAY
Story: Players are on a race track with many twists and turns. To begin the race, the coach introduces different signals: 'Green Flag' the players can dribble at any speed they wish; 'Red Flag' – there has been an accident and all cars must stop (foot on ball); 'Final Lap'– players must dribble at full speed. Add many other conditions to add turns, ball mastery skills etc. During the race, the carts need refuelling and new tires – go through the gates when coach shouts 'Pit Stop'. Coach/parent stands in between the cones to close the 'Pit Lane'.

COACHING NOTES
+ Coaching objectives – players dribbling with the laces and 'raise their heads' to see if a Pit Lane is closed or open.
+ Coaching tip – Add a points system to add extra excitement – 1pt for a Pit stop and change of direction.
+ Adaptations – numerous additional conditions can be added to increase or decrease difficulty, i.e. Add a Police Officer (player without the ball) to chase after speeding carts.

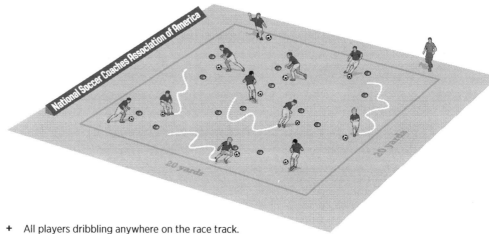

+ All players dribbling anywhere on the race track.
+ Introduce commands – i.e. 'Red Flag' - stop.

+ The coaches/parents have closed 3 of the 'Pit Lanes'.
+ Racing Carts must go to open 'Lanes' for a point.

+ Coaches/parents move in and out of the 'Pit Lanes'.
+ Players must find a different open pit.
+ Add 2 'Police Officers' to chase the speeding carts.

BEE HIVE

STAGES COVERED BY ACTIVITY
Stages 1, 2 & 3 - 3-11 year old players

THEMES & COMPETENCIES
Theme:
+ 1v1 attacking and defending
+ Dribbling
+ Ball mastery.

Competencies:
+ Turns and feints- basic
+ Dribbling basics
+ Fundamental movement skills
+ Beating and escaping an opponent
+ Attacking as an individual
+ Confidence and concentration
+ Defending as an individual.

WHY USE IT
'Bee Hive' is a small sided game emphasizing close control and dribbling with the laces. Coaches can introduce the speed of dribble, change of direction and simple attacking and defending strategies.

SET UP
15x15 yard square with Bee Hives - 3x3 yard squares marked with cones in each corner. 12 players organized into 4 teams – each team with a different colored training vest. At least 1 ball for each player.

HOW TO PLAY
Story: There are 4 Bee Hives close to a field of flowers with the Bee's favorite pollen. Each Bee has to supply the hive with 3 pollen balls to win the game. 4 teams of 3 'Bees'. Each Bee has a number (or a character name – Buzzy 1, 2 etc). Position each team behind one of the small corner squares (the hive). All the pollen balls are placed in the center of the playing area. The objective is to see which team can supply their hive with 3 pollen balls the quickest. The game starts with the coach shouting out a number. The activity can be progressed by reducing the number of balls in the center and allowing players to 'steal' from another hive.

COACHING NOTES
+ Coaching objectives – players dribbling with the laces and performing different turns when collecting the ball.
+ Coaching tip – Use assistant coaches/parents for 'crowd control' – helping keep players behind the hives and reminding players when it is their turn!
+ Adaptations – add balls to make the activity easier and reduce balls to create 1v1 duels.

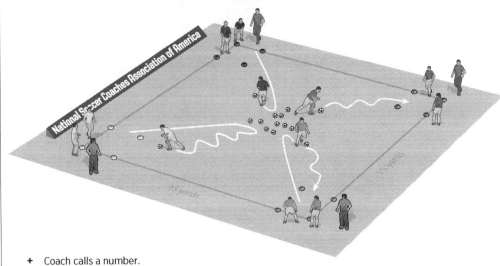

+ Coach calls a number.
+ The Bee with that number runs to the center of the 'field'.
+ The Bee dribbles one ball back to the hive

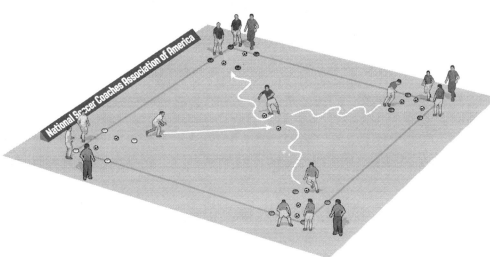

+ Coach can introduce different turns to retrieve the balls.
+ Keep returning to the 'field' to collect the pollen.

+ To progress the activity, reduce the number of balls in play.
+ Players steal pollen from other teams hive to collect 3.

PYRAMID CHALLENGE

STAGES COVERED BY ACTIVITY
Stages 1 & 2 - 3-8 year old players

THEMES & COMPETENCIES
Theme:
+ 1v1 attacking and defending
+ Dribbling
+ Ball mastery.

Competencies:
+ Turns and feints- basic
+ Dribbling basics
+ Fundamental movement skills
+ Beating and escaping an opponent
+ Attacking as an individual
+ Confidence and concentration
+ Defending as an individual.

WHY USE IT
In this fun and fast paced activity, the Egyptians (players) must avoid the Serpent Snake to build their pyramids. The dribbling activity also emphasizes take-on moves to beat a defender and is an opportunity for a coach to teach dribbling to space.

SET UP
15x20 yard area with an additional 5 yard end zone at one end. 14 balls of similar size are randomly placed in the end zone – each ball represents a 'pyramid stone'. All players start at the end of the area with a ball, facing the end zone. The 'Serpent Coach' stands in the middle of the area.

HOW TO PLAY
Story: The Egyptians are attempting to build a magnificent pyramid from stone situated at the end of the valley. The Egyptians must avoid the Serpent – at first without the ball – collect a stone and return back to the pyramid building site to build a 3 level and 14 ball pyramid (9 on the bottom, 4 on the next level and 1 on top). If the Serpent tags an Egyptian or touches a stone, the Egyptian becomes a Serpent. Egyptians win the game if they build a pyramid – they lose if the Serpent captures all the Egyptians before building the Serpent.

COACHING NOTES
+ Coaching objectives – players dribbling with the laces and performing different take-on moves to beat the 'Serpent'.
+ Coaching tip – Discuss with players Big Space and Little Space.
+ Adaptations – Players dribble balls in both directions, captured players go to the sides and fire (pass) boulders to hit the Egyptians below the knee.

+ Egyptians start at opposite end of the valley to the stones.
+ Serpent in the middle.
+ Egyptians start without a ball.

+ Egyptians avoid Serpent's tag.
+ On the return trip, Egyptians dribble the ball.
+ Egyptians build a 3 tiered pyramid.

+ Make cones wider to create more width.
+ Captured Egyptians pass boulders from the sides.

FETCH

STAGES COVERED BY ACTIVITY
Stages 1 & 2 - 3-8 year old players

THEMES & COMPETENCIES
Theme:
+ Dribbling
+ Ball mastery.

Competencies:
+ Turns and feints- basic
+ Dribbling basics
+ Fundamental movement skills
+ Beating and escaping an opponent

WHY USE IT
This activity is a great introduction to dribbling and ball mastery. Players are constantly moving and touching the ball – a fantastic way to activate the players at the beginning of the session.

SET UP
25 x 25 yard area with extra room to roam outside the square. Every player with a ball. 2-3 coaches/parent helpers.

HOW TO PLAY
The coach kneels down in the center of the area with the players around with their foot on the ball. The activity begins with the coach rolling a players ball out into the area – some long and some short. The player chases their ball and then dribbles the ball back to the coach. Involve a 2nd/3rd helper to ensure players are constantly moving. Repeat several times. Add challenges, such as:
+ The player must dribble to a different coach/helper each time,
+ The player has to catch the ball before it stops moving for a point,
+ Perform 5 toe taps before returning,
+ Left foot only,
+ Outside/heel only etc.

COACHING NOTES
+ Coaching objectives – the coach can add many different skills and objectives. Talk about the 10 surfaces of the feet – inside, outside, laces, heel and sole on each foot and perform moves with each.
+ Coaching tip – If coaching mixed ability groups, experiment ways to differentiate the activity to challenge all players.
+ Adaptations – alternate the serve height and direction and transition into another activity such as body part dribble or a tag game.

+ Players gather around the coach with a ball each.
+ Coach demonstrates some moves.

+ Coach rolls the balls randomly short and long.
+ Players chase, attempting to reach the ball before stopping.

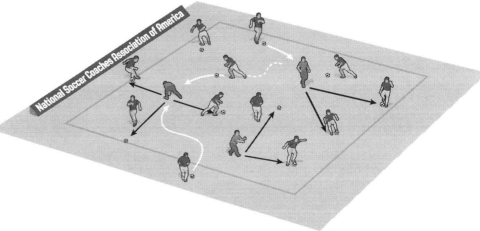

+ Additional coaches/parents join in.
+ Players alternate between servers.
+ Servers move to add an additional challenge.

CAN YOU?

STAGES COVERED BY ACTIVITY
Stages 1 & 2 - 3-8 year old players

THEMES & COMPETENCIES
Theme:
+ Dribbling
+ Ball mastery.

Competencies:
+ Turns and feints- basic
+ Dribbling basics
+ Fundamental movement skills
+ Beating and escaping an opponent

WHY USE IT
'Can You?' Is a terrific activity to commence a training session with young players and has almost endless variations and possibilities. The coach demonstrates an activity and asks the players – can you do that?

SET UP
25 x 25 yard area. 12 players each with a ball dribbling around the area.

HOW TO PLAY
Ask players to dribble around the area using the laces part of their shoe. After 1-2 mins, ask players to come close and place a foot on top of the ball. Explain how to play – the players must copy what the coach demonstrates. Start with fundamental movement skills such as running, skipping, galloping, balancing, dodging etc. Then introduce the ball and add new movements each time you play. E.g. 1) Dribble with laces - slow down and push the ball lightly with the laces - left, right and alternate. 2) Foundations – push the ball from side-to-side, right to the left foot and back again. 3) Toe taps – hopping from one foot to the other touching the top of the ball with the opposite foot each time. 4) Sole drag back – hopping between feet, move backwards dragging the ball back alternating between the sole of the shoes. 5) Sole push – push the ball forward with the sole of the shoes.

COACHING NOTES
+ Coaching objectives – the coach can add many different skills and objectives. Talk about the 10 surfaces of the feet – inside, outside, laces, heel and sole on each foot and perform moves with each.
+ Coaching tip – Start the activity without a ball and include fundamental movement skills.
+ Adaptations – the coach can add all sorts of movement patterns, turns and tricks to keep the game new and exciting for the players.

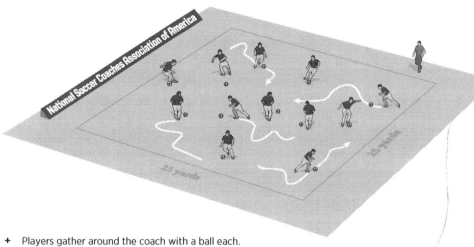

+ Players gather around the coach with a ball each.
+ Coach demonstrates some moves.

+ On the coach's command, players perform movement patterns.
+ Simple dribbling moves at first and then more challenging moves.

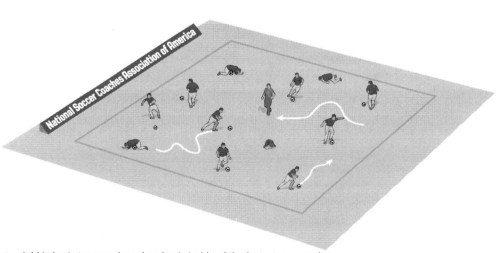

+ Add in basic turns such as drag back, inside of the foot, step-on and step-over.

BODY BALL

STAGES COVERED BY ACTIVITY
Stages 1 & 2 - 3-8 year old players

THEMES & COMPETENCIES
Theme:
+ Dribbling.
+ Ball mastery.

Competencies:
+ Turns and feints- basic.
+ Dribbling basics.
+ Fundamental movement skills.
+ Beating and escaping an opponent.

WHY USE IT
Young players like to experiment and 'Body Ball' is the perfect way to incorporate laughter and skill development into one activity. Players learn to use different surfaces of the feet and to keep hands off the soccer ball.

SET UP
25 x 25 yard area. 12 players each with a ball dribbling around the area.

HOW TO PLAY
Players dribble around the area listening for the coach's instruction. When the coach shouts out a body part, the players have to place that part on the ball. Start off simple, keeping the instruction to single body parts, such as, 'head', 'tummy' and 'bottom'. Increase the complexity by calling out 'left foot', 'right knee', 'left elbow' etc. As you know, some young players also like to use their hands. One way to introduce the 'no hands rule' is to have the players repeat as a group 'No hands in Soccer' when you call out 'hands' as a body part. Be ready for the smarty pants who tells you that goal keepers use their hands!

COACHING NOTES
+ Coaching objectives – To get the players moving and touching the ball using different parts of the foot. Also introduce players to 'left' and 'right' and the 'hand ball rule'.
+ Coaching tip – Kneel down so your head height is at the same level as your players to establish eye contact. Avoid wearing sunglasses when you coach.
+ Adaptations – As player's become more proficient, call out body parts consecutively (i.e. tummy, nose, elbow) or call out two body parts at once. (i.e. right hand and left foot).

+ Players dribble around the area listening for the coach to call a body part.
+ Start with simple parts such as tummy, bottom and head.

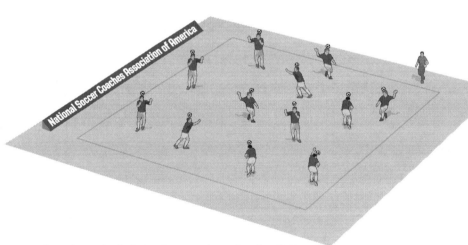

+ A good opportunity to teach some rules such as handball.
+ When coach says 'hands', plays repeat 'no hands in soccer'.

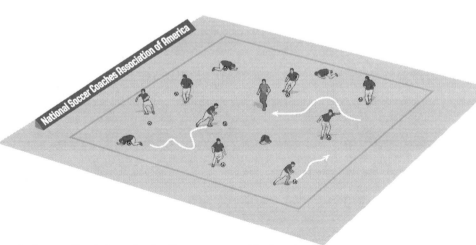

+ Increase the challenge by shouting a sequence of body parts.
+ Players need to place 2 body parts on the ball.

GOALS GALORE 1

STAGES COVERED BY ACTIVITY
Stages 1 & 2 - 3-8 year old players

THEMES & COMPETENCIES
Theme:
+ Dribbling
+ Ball mastery.
+ 1v1 Attacking and Defending
+ Shooting at an unopposed goal

Competencies:
+ Turns and feints- basic
+ Dribbling basics
+ Fundamental movement skills
+ Beating and escaping an opponent
+ Basic shooting technique

WHY USE IT
Even from an early age, young players love to score goals. As the name suggests, in this game players have many opportunities to enjoy scoring with and without pressure from an opponent.

SET UP
25 x 25 yard area. At least 1 ball per player and ideally several more. 4 teams each with 3 players. 4 sets of different colored training vests and 4 small portable goals placed centrally along each sideline.

HOW TO PLAY
4 teams, each with a coach/parent to assist, are positioned behind a cone in the 4 corners of the area. To begin, all the soccer balls are placed towards the center of the area, but not in a tight cluster. The coach starts the game by calling out a color – all the players from that team run out, collect a ball and score a goal. Allow 20 seconds per color so that all the players have a chance to score multiple goals. Coach then calls another color etc. Next, instruct the players that they cannot score in the same goal multiple times – try to score in all 4 goals. Finally, the coach rolls a ball into the area and the 3 players from the same team compete to score a goal.

COACHING NOTES
+ Coaching objectives – Enable players to experience scoring goals.
+ Coaching tip – Invest in a couple of sets of portable goals if the club does not provide them. Scoring goals is a major reason why players participate in the game.
+ Adaptations – In the final adaptation the coach can feed a new ball in continuously to enable all players to score a goal.

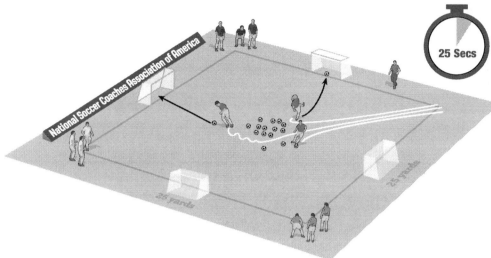

+ The red team is called by the coach.
+ Red players have 25 seconds to score as many goals as they can.

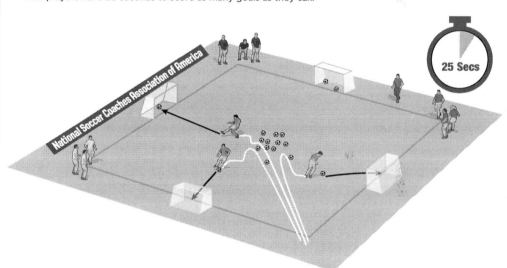

+ Add a condition that players must score in a different goal each time.

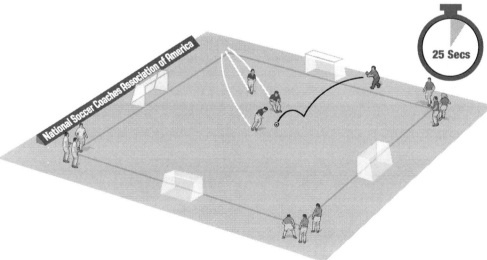

+ Use one ball served by the coach into the area.
+ 3 players from the same team compete to score.
+ Serve a new ball 2-3 times per group.

GOALS GALORE 2

STAGES COVERED BY ACTIVITY
Stages 1, 2 & 3 - 3-11 year old players

THEMES & COMPETENCIES
Theme:
+ Dribbling
+ Ball mastery.
+ 1v1 Attacking and Defending
+ Shooting at an unopposed goal

Competencies:
+ Turns and feints- basic
+ Dribbling basics
+ Fundamental movement skills
+ Beating and escaping an opponent
+ Basic shooting technique

WHY USE IT
Adding goals to practice sessions adds realism in the eyes of players and parents – it is the real game. Finishing a practice session with scoring goals is a perfect conclusion.

SET UP
25 x 25 yard area. At least 1 ball per player. 4 teams each with 3 players. 4 sets of colored vests. 2 small goals placed back to back and facing the outside of the area. Leave a 2 yard space between the goals.

HOW TO PLAY
2 teams of 3 players stand at each end of the grid facing each other. To maximize the time each player has participating, two parents/coaches start the game at the same time from each end. The coach kneels between the two lines with a pile of balls. 2 balls are rolled out into the area by the coach - first player from each line runs out to collect 1 ball before scoring. After a couple of attempts, change the pairings. Award 1 point to the first player to score in either goal. The third evolution involves 1 ball and 2 players competing to score. The final adaptation is to include the players from all 4 teams to compete for 1 or 2 balls.

COACHING NOTES
+ Coaching objectives – To eventually create 1v1 attacking and defending scenarios.
+ Coaching tip – To avoid disappointment, instruct the player scoring to return to their line and roll out another ball for the 2nd player to score an uncontested goal – everyone scores every time!
+ Adaptations – Once the players have learned a few moves/turns, instruct the players that before scoring they have to perform a move – such as an 'inside cut'.

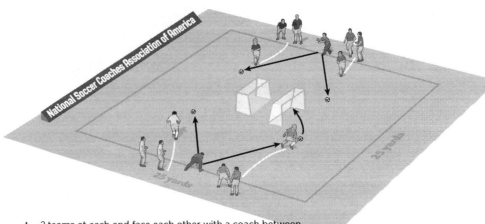

+ 2 teams at each end face each other with a coach between.
+ Coach serves 2 balls and each players attempts a shot.

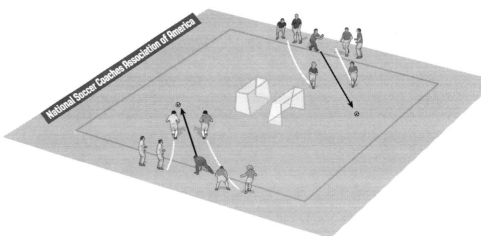

+ Each coach now serves 1 ball into the area.
+ Give both players an opportunity to score.

+ The players must perform a move before scoring.

DOCTOR DOCTOR

STAGES COVERED BY ACTIVITY
Stages 1 & 2 - 3-8 year old players

THEMES & COMPETENCIES
Theme:
+ Dribbling
+ Ball mastery.
+ 1v1 Attacking and Defending

Competencies:
+ Turns and feints- basic
+ Dribbling basics
+ Fundamental movement skills
+ Beating and escaping an opponent

WHY USE IT
The players love to play Doctor Doctor –
all players are constantly involved in this
game requiring team strategy!

SET UP
20x30 yard area. 1 ball per player. 2
teams of 6 players. 2 sets of different
colored training vests. Create 2 - 5x5
yard 'hospitals' at the end of the
rectangle at both ends.

HOW TO PLAY
Story – Children are playing in the school
yard and if they get injured, the school
Doctor is on hand to patch them up
and get them playing again. However,
without a Doctor there will be no one to
provide medical help.
Players are in 2 equal teams. 5 players
on each team dribble a ball in the
playground, weaving in and out of each
other. A Doctor in each team stands in
the 'hospital' waiting to be called. On
the command of 'GO', the 'school kids'
must attempt to pass their ball against an
opponent's ball. If a ball is hit, the player
is injured and must sit on his/her ball and
shout "DOCTOR DOCTOR". The Doctor
leaves the safety of the hospital and runs
to 'treat' the injured player (perform
a high-5). The injured player can now
resume dribbling. Once the Doctor leaves
the safety of the hospital, the opponents
can attempt to pass their ball to hit the
Doctor. The game ends if a DOCTOR is
hit or if all players are injured.

COACHING NOTES
+ Coaching objectives – Players must keep
  the ball moving to make it difficult for
  an opponent to hit their ball.
+ Coaching tip – It is often appropriate
  with young players for the coach to join
  in. In this activity, the coach can set the
  tone and intensity by being the Doctor.
+ Adaptations – Add a second doctor to
  keep the pace and action going.

+ Game commences with 2 teams dribbling.
+ Each team has a Doctor in the hospital.

+ Each teams attempt to injure their opponent.
+ The Doctor must leave the hospital to provide 'treatment'

+ The game is over when the Doctor has been hit.
+ Play again!

CROCODILE SWAMP

STAGES COVERED BY ACTIVITY
Stages 1 & 2 - 3-8 year old players

THEMES & COMPETENCIES
Theme:
+ Dribbling
+ Ball mastery.
+ 1v1 Attacking and Defending

Competencies:
+ Turns and feints- basic
+ Dribbling basics
+ Fundamental movement skills
+ Beating and escaping an opponent

WHY USE IT
'Crocodile Swamp' incorporates dribbling skills, changing direction and ball mastery. I great warm-up and activation activity.

SET UP
25x25 yard square and a smaller 10x10 yard square in the center. The smaller square is a 'no-go zone' and players should stay out until the coach instructs players to enter.

HOW TO PLAY
Story: Players are lost in a Floridian swamp full of crocodiles. As long as the players stay outside the swamp they are safe, but to score a point they must take a risk and cross the swamp and avoid a crocodile. To help the players become orientated and familiar with the activity, get the players dribbling in the large square. Introduce the direction of the dribble – left or right. Then, explain that the center square is the swamp – as the players dribble the coach calls 'Cross the Swamp' and the players must travel with the ball directly across one side to the other. Add different ways to change direction, moves to beat an opponent etc. Then add the 'Crocodile Coach' in the swamp and points for crossing the swamp without the Crocodile touching the ball. Play for up to ten minutes.

COACHING NOTES
+ Coaching objectives – Repetition and reinforcement of dribbling and ball mastery skills are essential– introduce inside and outside of the foot cut moves.
+ Coaching tip – At an early age teach players to perform cut moves using the correct foot and surface of the foot, so that the ball is furthest away from pressure.
+ Adaptations – Create a team game. Split the players into 4 teams of 3 players - 1 team are the crocodiles and the other 3 teams try to cross the swamp.

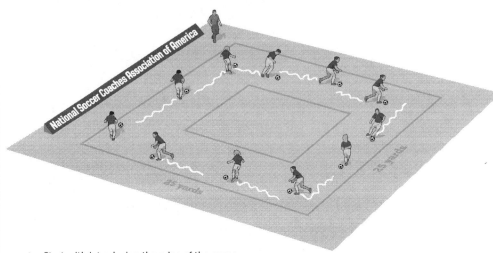

+ Start with introducing the rules of the game.
+ Players dribble inside the big square following the coach's commands.

+ Introduce the 'Swamp' and add the Crocodile.
+ Players earn a point each time they cross the swamp.
+ The Crocodile has to touch a ball.

+ Add 4 teams, 1 team are crocodiles in the swamp.
+ The other 3 teams have to cross using 'special moves'.

1V1 TO GOAL

STAGES COVERED BY ACTIVITY
Stages 1, 2 & 3 - 3-11 year old players

THEMES & COMPETENCIES
Theme:
+ Dribbling
+ Ball mastery.
+ 1v1 Attacking and Defending
+ Shooting at an unopposed goal

Competencies:
+ Turns and feints- basic
+ Dribbling basics
+ Beating and escaping an opponent
+ Basic shooting technique

WHY USE IT
1v1 to Goal gives players the chance to score a goal after they have performed an introductory move. The activity includes dribbling, take on moves and goal scoring.

SET UP
A 15x15 yard square with 2 goals on opposite sides, located centrally along the line. On the other 2 sides of the area, set up 2 cones opposite each other. Ideally, set up 2 areas to maximize the activity time for each player. 4 teams of 3 players with colored training vests – 2 teams in each area.

HOW TO PLAY
This activity is most appropriate for players that have progressed from introductory dribbling activities. Each team is situated behind a cone, facing each other. One team starts with the balls. The first player in the line dribbles towards the center of the square and the first player from the other line comes forward to defend. Once the dribbler goes through a cone gate, he/she can dribble towards either of the goals to the left or right. The defender attempts to win the ball and score in either goal.

COACHING NOTES
+ Coaching objectives – The goals are strategically placed to enable the coach to work with players on dribbling laterally and using different cut moves before scoring.
+ Coaching tip – Utilize assistant coaches to occasionally split the group so players receive more involvement and touches.
+ Adaptations – Although passing is not a key focus at the first stage, give players an opportunity to experience playing as a 'team' – 2v2 – 1 ball.

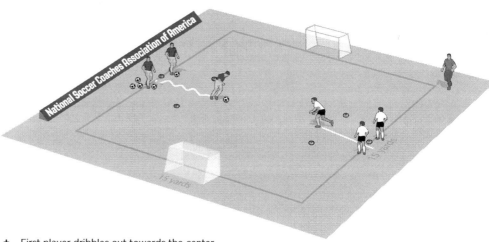

+ First player dribbles out towards the center.
+ The dribbler must pass through the gate before scoring.

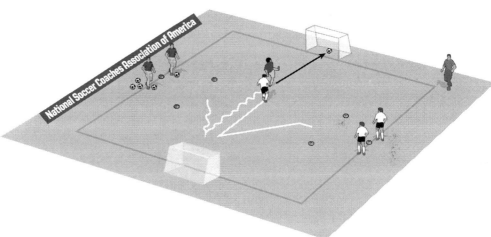

+ Player encouraged to use 'cut' moves to change direction.
+ Work with players to use a move to keep ball away from pressure.

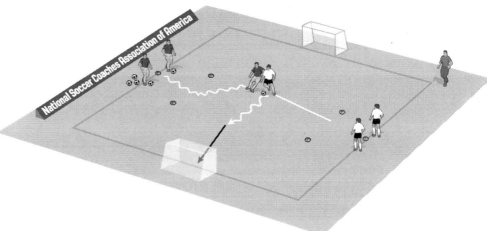

+ If the defender wins the ball, he/she can score.

CAT AND MOUSE

STAGES COVERED BY ACTIVITY
Stages 1 & 2 - 3-8 year old players

THEMES & COMPETENCIES
Theme:
+ Dribbling
+ Ball mastery.
+ 1v1 Attacking and Defending

Competencies:
+ Turns and feints- basic
+ Dribbling basics
+ Beating and escaping an opponent

WHY USE IT
Cat and mouse introduces young players to some simple 1v1 concepts, such as the need to keep the ball (attacking) and win the ball from an opponent (defending).

SET UP
25x25 yard square with 4 small 2 yard squares 2 yards from the corners (use 2 different colored cones). 3 teams with 4 players in colored training vests. Players from 2 teams have soccer balls (mice) and 1 team without the balls (cats). Additional 16 training vests – place 2 in each mini square (mouse hole).

HOW TO PLAY
Story: The 'Cats' are chasing after the mice and trying to catch their tails (training vests tucked into the shorts of the mice). The mice can dribble to a mouse hole, where they are safe from the cat. The mouse can only stay in the mouse hole for 5 seconds at a time (use parents to help move the mice along). If a mouse loses its tail, they can dribble their ball to a mouse hole to retrieve a new tail. Once all the tails have gone from the mouse holes, start a new game with new cats.

COACHING NOTES
+ Coaching objectives – Instruct the players to keep the ball moving – standing still helps a defender. Dribble to space and away from pressure.
+ Coaching tip – Young players will have difficulty placing their own tails in their shorts – get parents to help – or players hold the pinnie and the cat has to tag the player to get the tail.
+ Adaptations – To make it more difficult for the mice, reduce the mouse holes to 2-3. If the tag game is going too quickly, make the 'tagger' dribble a ball to slow them down.

+ 2 teams of mice dribble the balls.
+ 1 team of cats without balls chase the mice.
+ Parents help the coach.

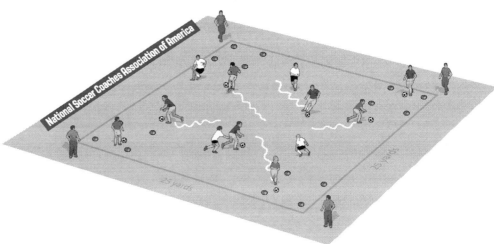

+ Mice are safe when in the mice hole.
+ There are new tails for mice in the mice hole.
+ Cats pull out the mice tails.

+ Remove 2 mice holes to make it more difficult for the mice.

1V1 TO 3V3 NUMBERS GAME

STAGES COVERED BY ACTIVITY
Stages 1, 2 & 3 - 3-11 year old players

THEMES & COMPETENCIES
Theme:
+ Dribbling
+ Ball mastery.
+ 1v1 Attacking and Defending
+ Shooting at an unopposed goal

Competencies:
+ Turns and feints- basic
+ Dribbling basics
+ Beating and escaping an opponent
+ Basic shooting technique

WHY USE IT
The numbers game is a young player classic and a stable activity for coaches introducing game concepts, rules and basic attacking and defending principles.

SET UP
The shape and configuration of the area can be adapted in many different ways. For this activity, use a rectangle 25x15 yards with a small goal at each end to form a traditional soccer field shape.

HOW TO PLAY
To maximize the player's involvement in the game, set up to adjoining areas, with 6 to 8 players in each area. With 12 players in the same area, create 4 teams of 3 players in the same color pinnies. Assign a team to each corner - solicit the help of a parent/coach. Number the players 1-3 and try to match the playing ability of the players. Keep a good supply of balls and give each group approximately 30 seconds before changing the number. When the coach shouts out '1' the players with that number run out into the area and attempt to score a goal. If the ball goes out of play, shout 'NEW BALL' and serve a new ball into the area. When a player scores, send them back to their team and then serve a new ball for the remaining players - this way everyone gets to score. Progress to a 2v2 and 3v3.

COACHING NOTES
+ Coaching objectives – balance the ability levels to give players a challenge.
+ Coaching tip – introduce rules and objectives of 'the' game.
+ Adaptations – Change the shape of the area, add more goals, add rules for older players such as the need to make a pass before scoring, etc.

+ Teams start in the 4 corners of the area.
+ Parent helpers assist the coach.
+ Coach rolls a ball into the area and calls a number.

+ A player from each team competes for the ball.
+ Players attempt to score.
+ Coach sends a goal scorer back to their line.

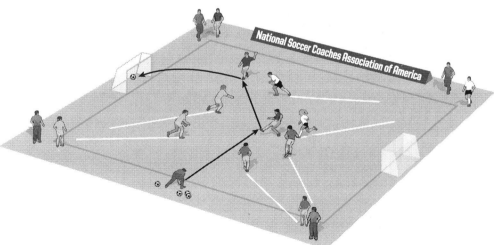

+ Progress to calling 2 numbers.
+ Add a condition that players must pass once before scoring.

SNOOKER

STAGES COVERED BY ACTIVITY
Stages 1, 2 & 3 - 3-11 year old players

THEMES & COMPETENCIES
Theme:
+ Dribbling
+ Ball mastery.
+ 1v1 Attacking and Defending

Competencies:
+ Turns and feints- basic
+ Dribbling basics
+ Beating and escaping an opponent

WHY USE IT
This activity follows the popular pastime 'Snooker', or for an American audience the game can be called 'Pool'. Using a number of turns and dribbling moves, players attempt to score points!

SET UP
A rectangle, 25x15 yards. In the four corners, create a 'pocket', using flags or cones 2 yards apart. Add 2 additional 'pockets' in the center of the long sides. Set up 2 areas, so that the players are on task continuously.

HOW TO PLAY
In each area, play 3v3, with the purpose to 'pot' (pass or dribble) 8 balls into any of the 6 pockets to win the game. If possession turns over, immediately switch roles and continue play. A few variations to make this activity appropriate for 3-year-old and older players. Diagram 1: instruct team 1 to find a space in the area and stand like a statue (they cannot move). The coach rolls a ball to a player on the other team, who is allowed 3 touches to 'pot' into any 'pocket'. Give each player an opportunity and then change roles. Diagram 2: allow the defenders to move, but they must link arms to slow them down. Diagram 3: alternate serve, with no restrictions on the defenders. If a ball is 'potted' the team retains possession from the coach's serve.

COACHING NOTES
+ Coaching objectives – players start to appreciate 'big-space' and 'small-space'. Overly encourage dribbling and limit your urge to require passing!
+ Coaching tip – differentiate the environment by adapting the rules, personnel and layout based on your assessment of success.
+ Adaptations – play 3 attackers v 1 defender. Defenders tag in and out on the call of CHANGE. Time how long it takes a team to pot 8 balls and then switch.

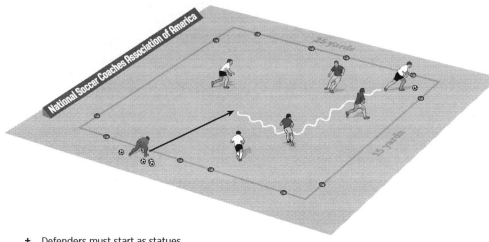

+ Defenders must start as statues.
+ Attackers can dribble or pass.
+ 3 touch restriction.

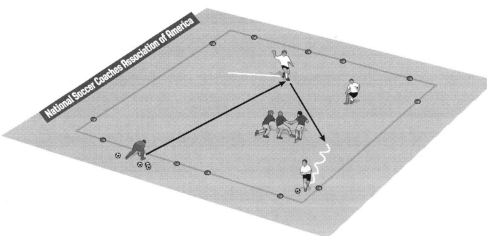

+ Defenders move, but with linked arms.
+ Ask players to identify 'big space' and 'small space'.

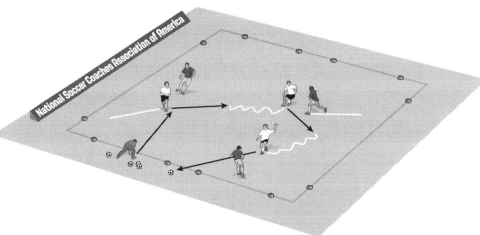

+ Progress to 3v3 with no defensive restrictions.

FREEZE

STAGES COVERED BY ACTIVITY
Stages 1 & 2 - 3-8 year old players

THEMES & COMPETENCIES
Theme:
+ Dribbling
+ Ball mastery.
+ 1v1 Attacking and Defending

Competencies:
+ Turns and feints- basic
+ Dribbling basics
+ Beating and escaping an opponent

WHY USE IT
'Freeze' is a tag game involving all the players dribbling, dodging and using moves to allude Mr Freeze.

SET UP
Set up a square, 25x25 yards. A ball and a vest per player.

HOW TO PLAY
Story: Mr Freeze is a super hero and protects the people from a terrible virus spreading through 'Ice City'. The only way Mr/Mrs Freeze can stop the virus is to freeze it.
Start without balls, so the players can get accustomed to the rules. Select 2 players to be Mr/Mrs Freeze, who stand outside the area. All the other players are in space in the area, wearing a vest. When the coach shouts 'FREEZE THEM', Mr/Mrs Freeze chase the players around the area. If a 'virus' is tagged (frozen) or leaves the area, they must stand with their feet wide apart and hands on their head. A virus can be thawed out when another virus crawls between their legs. Once all virus are frozen, the game is over and a new game is started. As soon as the players are adequately familiar with the activity, add balls. A frozen 'virus' picks up the ball and places on his/her head with legs apart. To unfreeze a virus, pass the ball between the legs.

COACHING NOTES
+ Coaching objectives – to get players moving and aware of opponents and teammates.
+ Coaching tip – Young players often leave the playing area in their excitement. To help them understand the perimeter, play follow the leader and walk around the area.
+ Adaptations – Add a time limit, record the best time, increase the number of 'Mr/Mrs Freeze' and if necessary, join in to help Mr/Mrs Freeze.

+ The virus runs around the area with a ball.
+ 2 players are Mr/Mrs Freeze.
+ If tagged, stand with legs apart.

+ Add the balls.
+ Frozen virus are released by passing through their legs.

+ Coach joins in to help Mr/Mrs Freeze.
+ Add a time limit!

FLIP 'EM

STAGES COVERED BY ACTIVITY
Stages 1 & 2 - 3-8 year old players

THEMES & COMPETENCIES
Theme:
+ Dribbling.
+ Ball mastery.

Competencies:
+ Turns and feints- basic.
+ Dribbling basics.

WHY USE IT
'Flip 'em' is a terrific warm-up exercise that incorporates fundamental movement skills and can include the ball.

SET UP
Set up a square, 25x25 yards. A ball per player and 2 sets of colored vests. 20+ small hat cones – 50% right side up and 50% right side down.

HOW TO PLAY
Separate the players into 2 teams. Set the cones randomly in the area, so the cones are spread evenly. One team has to turn all the cones right side up and the other team turns all the cones right side down. On the command of 'GO' players rush out into the area and start 'flipping' the cones. Play for a minute and then count how many cones are up and how many are down. Play a couple of times, then give each player a ball. Now, the players must perform the same activity, but must dribble a ball whilst flipping the cones. Increase the time to 2 minutes when introducing the ball.

COACHING NOTES
+ Coaching objectives – activate the players focus and enthusiasm towards the activity.
+ Coaching tip – Choose the right activities according to the weather and time of day – tag games involving all players and games like Flip 'em are perfect for cold days and late afternoon sessions.
+ Adaptations – add 2-3 different colored cones and give them different point values, i.e. red cone 1 point and blue cone 2 points.

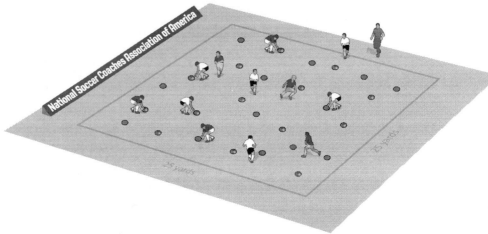

+ Players flip over the cones.
+ 1 minute intervals and count the cones

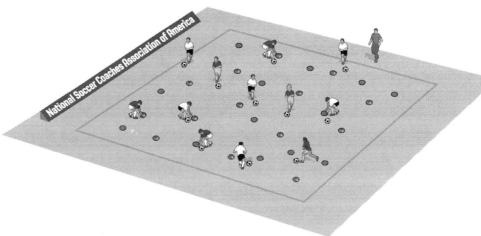

+ Players must now dribble the ball.
+ Add extra time as movements will be much slower.

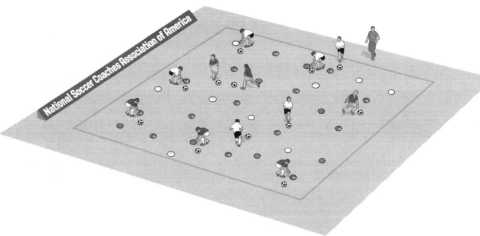

+ Add in some different colored cones.
+ Red cones 1 point and blue cones 2 points.

LOOTERS

STAGES COVERED BY ACTIVITY
Stages 1 & 2 - 3-8 year old players

THEMES & COMPETENCIES
Theme:
+ Dribbling.
+ Ball mastery.
+ 1v1 Attacking and Defending.

Competencies:
+ Turns and feints- basic.
+ Dribbling basics.
+ Beating and escaping an opponent.

WHY USE IT
Looters is a great opportunity to introduce new turns and take on moves. As the number of balls decrease, 1v1 and 2v1 scenarios pop up all over the area.

SET UP
A rectangle, 30x20 yards. Create 2x5 yard 'home' boxes at either end of the area. A ball per player and 2 sets of colored vests.

HOW TO PLAY
2 equal teams standing inside their own 'home' box. Balls are lined up between the 2 side lines across the center of the area. On the command of "GO" players leave their square and attempt to dribble a ball back to their 'home'. An opponent cannot challenge for the ball in the first version of the activity. Play until all balls are in either of the two squares. Modify the rules to progress the activity, i.e. 1) Players can compete to win possession, 2) Players can enter the opponents 'home' box to steal the balls (90 second time limit), 3) Split each team into attackers and defenders – each cannot enter the other half of the field and must pass to get the ball back to the home area, 4) Create equal numbers of small 'home' squares around the area – once the ball enters this area the ball cannot be removed.

COACHING NOTES
+ Coaching objectives – This activity offers opportunities to discuss with young players basic attacking and defending concepts.
+ Coaching tip – Use guided discovery methods to draw out solutions from the young players, such as 'how can you stop the other team?'
+ Adaptations – This game can be modified by creating 3-4 teams.

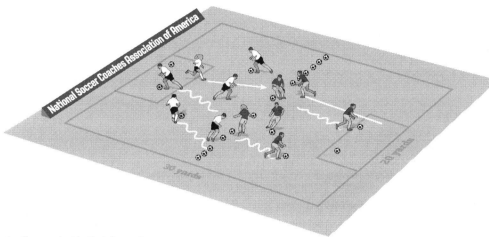

+ Teams start in their home box.
+ No tackling to begin.
+ Team with most balls in home box wins.

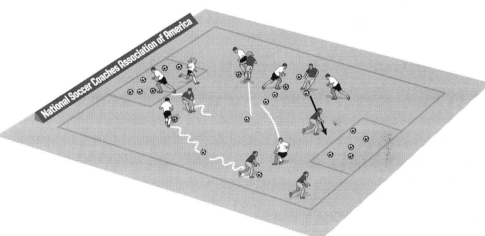

+ Progress to players competing for possession.
+ 1v1 and 2v1 situations in abundance.

+ Add a center line.
+ Split each team into attackers and defenders.
+ Defenders cannot cross center, so must pass to attackers.

RUNAWAY ROBOTS

STAGES COVERED BY ACTIVITY
Stages 1 & 2 - 3-8 year old players

THEMES & COMPETENCIES
Theme:
+ Dribbling.
+ Ball mastery.
+ 1v1 Attacking and Defending.

Competencies:
+ Turns and feints- basic.
+ Dribbling basics.
+ Beating and escaping an opponent.

WHY USE IT
This fun activity is a great way to involve parents and an opportunity to find your next coach!

SET UP
25x25 yard square to form 'Soccer Space'. 12 players each with a ball are the Space Rangers. 5-12 parent Robots.

HOW TO PLAY
The Story: Runaway Robots are on the loose in Soccer Space. It's up to the Space Rangers (players) to try and destroy the robots using their Space Lasers (ball). Before starting the game, perform an active demonstration of the rules. The Robots must move like Robots – slow and stiff. The objective is to hit the Robots with the ball – 5 hits leading to the Robot's demise: 1) Robot loses power in their right arm (right arm behind the back). 2) Lose power to the left arm (both arms behind the back). 3) Lose right leg (hop on one leg). 4) Lose left leg (kneeling). 5) Complete shut-down (lie on the ground). Start the game - Space Rangers moving around with their Laser in Soccer Space firing them at the Robots. Stop occasionally to identify operating Robots. After the 5th hit, Robots either lay on the ground or leave Soccer Space.

COACHING NOTES
+ Coaching objectives – After the first round, ask the players what they do to fire their lasers hard at the Robots. Focus on using laces and toe pointed down.
+ Coaching tip – Task each player with getting a parent guardian to be a Robot. A good way to identify your next parent coach!
+ Adaptations – Flip the roles. Parents are Space Rangers and players Robots. Remind parents to strike the ball softly.

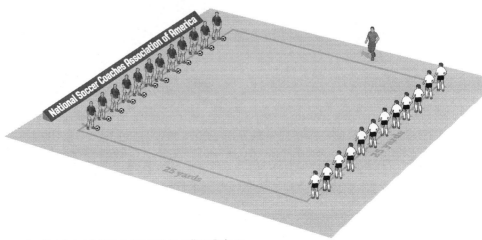

+ Coach sends Space Rangers to collect Robots.
+ Robots stand at one end of the area Rangers at the other.

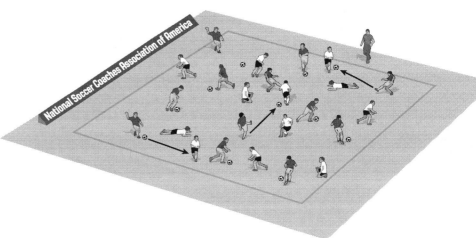

+ Rangers fire lasers at the Robots.
+ Robots go down in 5 stages.

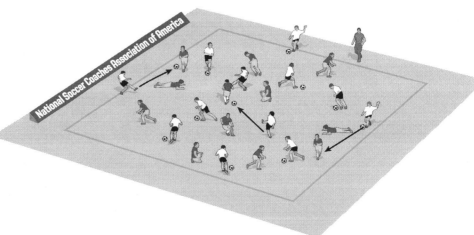

+ Flip the roles – Rangers become Robots.

SLEEPING GIANT

STAGES COVERED BY ACTIVITY
Stages 1 & 2 - 3-8 year old players

THEMES & COMPETENCIES
Theme:
+ Dribbling.
+ Ball mastery.
+ 1v1 Attacking and Defending.

Competencies:
+ Turns and feints - basic.
+ Dribbling basics.
+ Beating and escaping an opponent.

WHY USE IT
Coach plays a pivotal role to keep the activity going and fun. Dribbling with 'head-up' helps players steal the treasure.

SET UP
Set up a Giant's and Villagers area about 20 yards apart – does not need to be in a square. Use flags for the giant's area so players feel like they are sneaking inside. A ball per player and 2-3 sets of vests.

HOW TO PLAY
The Story: The giant has stolen all the villagers treasure. The villagers know the giant always falls asleep when he hears his favourite song. The villagers come up with a sneaky plan to send the giant into a deep sleep by singing his/her favourite song, such as Twinkle Twinkle Little Star. Once the giant is asleep the villagers may dribble their ball toward the giant and the treasure. If the giant stirs, the villagers must hide behind their ball. Once again the villagers must send the giant back to sleep by singing. When asleep, villagers can dribble the ball closer. Once a villager gets inside the giants cave, they can take a piece of treasure and return to their village. The aim is to win back all the treasure. The Giant may wake up, chase and capture the villagers - they become a 'little giant'.

COACHING NOTES
+ Coaching objectives – Players learn to dribble and look up at the same time.
+ Coaching tip – Working with 3-5 year old players requires energy and goofiness, singing nursery rhymes is part of the deal! Enjoy it – kids will love you for it and so will the parents.
+ Adaptations – Lay out the color vests, for example all Red (Rubies). Once the villagers have stolen back the rubies lay out your Yellow vests (Gold).

+ The giant is sleeping in his/her cave.
+ The villagers approach slowly and quietly.

+ Villagers enter the cave and steal back treasure.
+ If the Giant wakes sing him/her back to sleep.

+ The giant may chase the villagers back to the village.
+ Captured villagers become little giants.

STAGE 2: PLAYERS 6-8 YEARS OLD

STAGE 2 - **MIDDLE CHILDHOOD (6-8 YEARS OLD)**

A 6 year old is eager, active and likes to be on the go. Although keen to act independently, a 6 year old needs parental approval, understanding, praise and encouragement. Pushing too hard or expecting too much can result in the child becoming tense and nervous. An 8 year old is able to accept moderate responsibilities. Peer groups become important and the child will identify with other youngsters of the same sex and with similar interests and activities.

DEVELOPMENT FOCUS
- Movement skills and technical development remain top of the agenda in Stage 2.
- Small sided games and teamwork activities are introduced.
- Speed training commences for Girls (6-8 years) and Boys (7-9 years)
- Optimal time for training suppleness occurs for both Girls and Boys in stages 2 and 3 (6-10 years)

KEY DEVELOPMENT POINTS FOR CHILDREN IN STAGE 2

Physically	Psychological/Social	Cognitive/Mental
1. Coordination and body control improve rapidly as there is slower growth.	1. Interests often change rapidly.	1. Imaginative, spontaneous and creative.
2. Boys and girls have equal ability.	2. Enjoys initiating activities.	2. Able to stay on task longer due to increased attention span.
3. Reaction time is slow, but improves as the child grows.	3. Enjoys being praised for endeavors from adults.	3. Likes to be tested but often dislikes public failure.
4. Lots of energy as endurance levels but there are fluctuations in energy.	4. Starts to become more independent and attempts to exercise more control over own environment.	4. Likes to try new activities.
5. High need for skill development.	5. Appreciates consistency in own environment.	5. Better able to understand and learn because of growing memory capacity.
6. Fine motor skills developing.	6. Learns by repetition.	6. Starting to visualize instructions –although demonstrations are much more concrete.
7. Visual and hand/eye coordination improving.	7. Experimental, exploratory behavior is part of development.	7. Inconsistent attention span.
8. Height and weight increasing at a steady rate.	8. Still egocentric – each player wants a ball.	8. Interests can be short and fast changing.
9. Balance improves with ear developments.	9. Peer group becomes increasingly important.	9. Highly verbal.
10. Learns best by being physically active.	10. Players are concrete thinkers and find abstract concepts difficult.	10. Asks fact-orientated questions (e.g., wants to know how, why and when).
11. Needs to repeat activities that are well known and mastered.	11. Players start to develop powers of reasoning – if you do 'X' the result will be 'Y'.	11. Rapid development of mental skills.
12. Eye development and ability to track objects in motion improving.	12. Easily motivated and eager to try something new. Willingness to seek risk and adventure.	12. Greater ability to describe experiences and talk about thoughts and feelings.
13. High center of gravity, so balance can be difficult.	13. Needs guidance and praise from adults to stay on task and to achieve the best performance.	13. Less focus on one's self – seeks social comparison.
	14. Increasingly self-assured but can be childish and silly at times.	
	15. Stronger sense of right and wrong.	
	16. Growing desire to be liked and accepted by friends.	
	17. Enthusiastic and impatient.	

DEVELOPMENT CHARACTERISTICS TRANSLATED TO COACHING PLAYERS IN STAGE 2

TRANSLATED TO PLAYER DEVELOPMENT THIS MEANS

1. Continued involvement of fundamental movement skills – running, jumping, skipping, throwing etc

2. Focusing on ball familiarization and dribbling skills – one ball per child.

3. Introduction of paired and cooperation activities.

4. Help players understand a task by demonstration and asking questions

5. Sessions requiring players to be extremely active.

6. Selecting activities that do not place undue stress on the muscles, bones and energy systems of the body.

7. Repeating activities regularly – constant change and insufficient reinforcement negatively affects learning

8. Camouflaging and concealing technical information by using names, characters and stories.

9. Encouraging trial and error, keeping instruction to a minimum

10. Using equipment and props to increase complexity but continue to make the sessions fun – hurdles, hoops, ladders, bean bags, etc.

11. Including competitive games, but emphasize success other than just winning (i.e. effort)

12. Providing considerable encouragement.

13. Including 'games and matches' in every session

14. Introduction to small sided games – 2 v 2 to 4 v 4 – play at the end of a practice session – don't sacrifice practice sessions for games at this stage.

15. All players to receive fundamental goal keeping skills – catching, throwing and diving (players love to dive!).

16. Introduce basic rules of the game – including restarts when ball leaves the field.

17. Passing skills can be introduced.

18. Avoiding temptation to place players in specialist positions (i.e. full back, forward or goal keeper)

ISLAND DRIBBLING

STAGES COVERED BY ACTIVITY
Stages 2 & 3 - 6-11 year old players

THEMES & COMPETENCIES
Theme:
+ Dribbling and turns.
+ Attacking as an individual.
+ Defending as an individual.

Competencies:
+ Dribbling basics.
+ Turning basics.
+ Feints and dribble.
+ Beating an opponent.
+ Escaping an opponent.

WHY USE IT
This activity develops player's confidence - using moves to beat a defender and improving player's vision

SET UP
20x25 playing area marked with cones in the corners. Use three cones to make a triangle or island and create 8 islands in the grid. Each player will start with a ball.

HOW TO PLAY
The first few rounds of play the players will try to dribble through as many islands as possible in 45 seconds. In subsequent rounds player will have to perform a move to beat or escape a defender in the center of the island: such as inside cut, scissor, step over, etc.

COACHING NOTES
+ Main coaching objectives – develop confidence on the ball and quickness when performing moves.
+ Coaching tips – the triangle/island encourages players to dribble in one side and out another side. Emphasize that players should accelerate after the move.
+ Adaptations – add two 'taggers' in the final stage to increase difficulty

+ Players look to dribble through islands as fast as possible in 45 seconds.
+ Can players improve on their last score?

+ Players now need to perform a move in the center of the island.
+ Coach can tell them the first few moves and then ask the players to come up with their own moves.

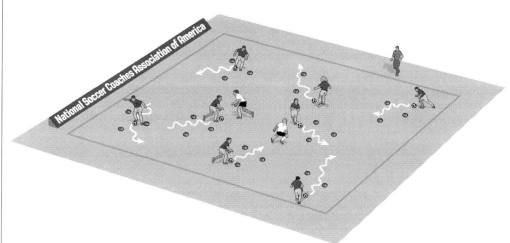

+ Have two players try to win the ball from those that are dribbling.
+ Once they win the ball they drop the training vest.
+ Players may stop on an island and are safe for 5 seconds from taggers.

FRUIT SALAD

STAGES COVERED BY ACTIVITY
Stages 2 & 3 - 6-11 year old players

THEMES & COMPETENCIES
Theme:
+ Dribbling and turns.

Competencies:
+ Physical literacy skills.
+ Dribbling basics.
+ Turning basics.
+ Feints and dribble.

WHY USE IT
This activity is designed to get players to dribble with their head up and also use different surfaces of the foot to dribble.

SET UP
15x15 playing area marked with cones in the corners. There are 16 cones scattered throughout the grid. The cones are yellow, red, orange, and purple. Each of the 12 players will need a ball for the second phase. The coach also has one cone of each color in her hand.

HOW TO PLAY
Players start out performing different movements between the cones as a warm-up. Players then must dribble inside the grid and avoid the cones. The coach will hold a cone up and have the players call out a fruit of that color. The players will progress from dribbling with different surfaces, to performing stationary moves at a cone, and then moves to beat a player.

COACHING NOTES
+ Main coaching objectives – develop player's vision and comfort on the ball.
+ Coaching tips – you can make the space smaller to make it more difficult for players or enlarge the grid to make it easier.
+ Adaptations – have another coach or parent also hold up cones so players have more than one person to look out for while dribbling.

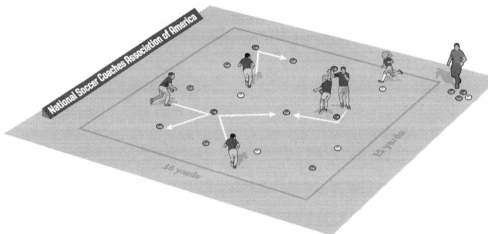

+ Coach calls out a movement for players to perform.
+ Coach can ask players to give "high fives" to teammates.

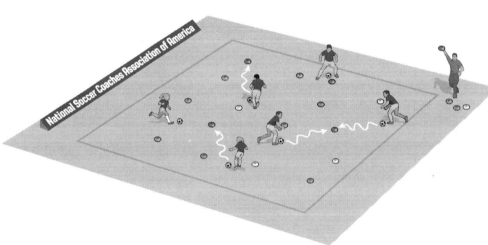

+ When the coach raises a cone the players have to call out a fruit of that color.
+ Payers dribble to a cone and perform 6 reps of a stationary move, i.e. toe touches.

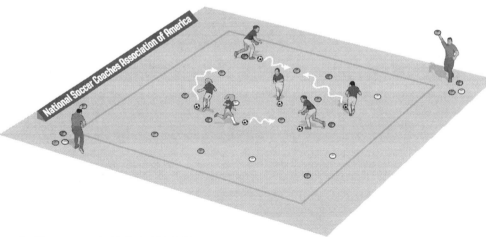

+ Players now accelerate to the cone.
+ Have a coach or parent also hold up cones.

PIRATES TREASURE

THEMES & COMPETENCIES
Theme:
+ Dribbling and turns.
+ Attacking as an individual.
+ Defending as an individual.

Competencies:
+ Dribbling basics.
+ Turning basics.
+ Feints and dribble.
+ Beating an opponent.
+ Escaping an opponent.

WHY USE IT
This game incorporates dribbling moves to beat a defender, turning, and body coordination.

SET UP
15x20 playing area marked with cones in the corners. 24 cones (gold) are positioned at the end of the grid (island). Each player with a ball will start on the opposite side of the grid. The coach is in the middle of the grid.

HOW TO PLAY
Players must dribble past the coach in the middle who acts as passive defender. When the players get to the treasure area, they must pick up one piece of gold and dribble back to the end line. Once all the gold is picked up the players can then dribble down with it and bury it back on the island.

COACHING NOTES
+ Main Coaching Objectives – Players should look to time their moves to beat the coach. Players should recognize the cues to take long touches to attack space vs short touches to set up a move.
+ Coaching tips – if there is not enough space have players dribble in two waves instead of one.
+ Adaptations – add more defenders who can win the ball

+ Players must perform a move while dribbling to get to the treasure.
+ The coach acts as a passive defender as the players try to dribble to the island.

+ The coach can now defend.
+ Players should recognize when they have space to take bigger touches.

+ Have 1-2 players act as defenders.
+ Once a dribbler loses her ball she joins the defenders.

LINE DRIBBLE

STAGES COVERED BY ACTIVITY
Stages 2 & 3 - 6-11 year old players

THEMES & COMPETENCIES
Theme:
+ Dribbling and turns.
+ Passing and receiving.
+ Attacking as an individual.
+ Defending as an individual.

Competencies:
+ Dribbling basics.
+ Turning basics.
+ Feints and dribble.
+ Beating an opponent.
+ Escaping an opponent.
+ Passing over a short distance.
+ Receiving the ball with the feet.
+ Shooting technique.

WHY USE IT
This game is designed to give players repetition using moves to beat a defender.

SET UP
20x25 playing area marked with cones in the corners. Cones are also laid 5 yards off each end line to create end zones. Flags are also placed 10 yards from the center of the sideline where the coach stands. Players are split into two teams of six and each team wears a different colored vest. The coach is on the touchline with all the balls.

HOW TO PLAY
When the coach says, "Go" the first person in each line must run down to the flag on their side before entering the field. The coach plays a ball towards one player to create an attacking advantage. The player must dribble to the opposite end zone and stop the ball for a point. If the defending player wins the ball, she can score at the opposite line.

COACHING NOTES
+ Main coaching objectives – players need to make a good first touch and attack the defender at speed.
+ Coaching tips – if the groups take too much time you can play a 2nd ball out for the next group to play simultaneously.
+ Adaptations – start to add numbers to the activity to create 2v1, 2v2, and 3v2 games

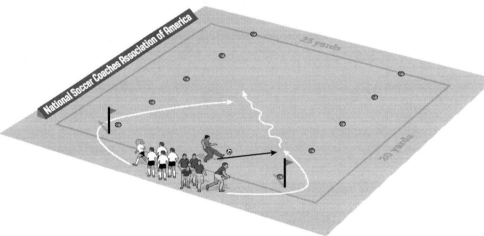

+ Coach says "Go" and first person in each line runs around their flag.
+ Player who last touched the ball brings it back to the coach.

+ Coach can now call out more than one player from a team, for example: "2 blue and 1 white."
+ Have players leave the ball if it goes out of bounds or if they score.

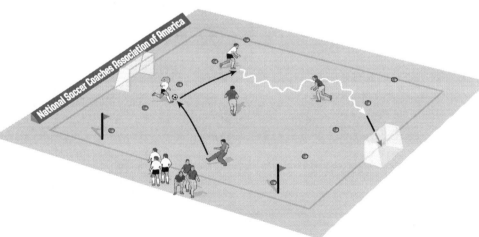

+ Add a small goal at either end.
+ The coach talks with the players while they wait in line to play.

SIX GOAL GAME

STAGES COVERED BY ACTIVITY
Stages 2 & 3 - 6-11 year old players

THEMES & COMPETENCIES
Theme:
+ Dribbling and turns.
+ Passing and receiving.
+ Attacking as an individual.
+ Defending as an individual.

Competencies:
+ Dribbling basics.
+ Turning basics.
+ Feints and dribble.
+ Beating an opponent.
+ Escaping an opponent.
+ Passing over a short distance.
+ Receiving the ball with the feet.

WHY USE IT
Using multiple goals allows for players to keep their heads up and find other scoring options. Players can dribble to penetrate to goal or recognize when to change direction.

SET UP
30x35 playing area marked with cones in the corner. 3 goals that are 2 yards wide are created on each end-line with cones. 12 players are placed on 3 teams, each with a different training vest. Soccer balls are with the coach on the side.

HOW TO PLAY
2 teams will play 4 vs 4 on the field and a third team acts as bumpers on the touch line. Teams will play for 2 minutes and then the bumper team will switch with a team on the field. The coach is the "boss of the ball" and restarts each game with a pass.

COACHING NOTES
+ Main coaching objectives – decision making of when to dribble to penetrate; vision to see scoring options.
+ Coaching tips – play more than one ball in to get more players involved
+ Adaptations - instead of acting like bumpers the third team can stand behind the goals as gate keepers who take turns stepping into goals to close them off.

+ Coach plays the ball in any time a goal is scored or a ball goes out of bounds.
+ Teams may play to the bumper team for support.

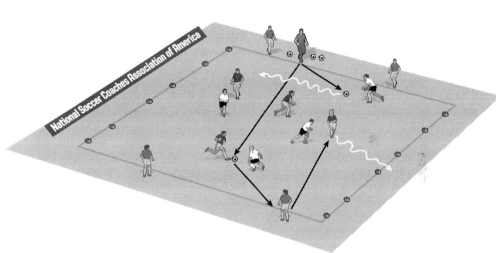

+ If there are players that are not active, the coach may play in an additional ball.
+ Coach should remind bumper players to move to support the play.

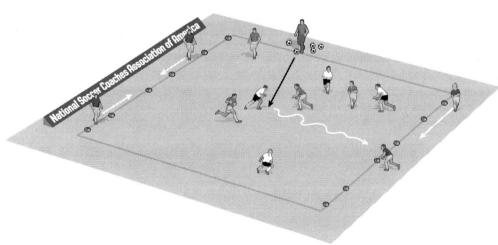

+ To increase the difficulty of the activity, allow the resting team to act as gate keepers for the goals.
+ They may step in and close off goals at varying times.

CATEGORIES

STAGES COVERED BY ACTIVITY
Stages 2 & 3 - 6-11 year old players

THEMES & COMPETENCIES
Theme:
+ Dribbling and turns.
+ Passing and receiving.

Competencies:
+ Dribbling basics.
+ Turning basics.
+ Feints and dribble.
+ Beating an opponent.
+ Passing over a short distance.
+ Receiving the ball with the feet.

WHY USE IT
Teach players how to angle their run and receive a ball

SET UP
8x8 square in the center of a large circle of players. Players are split in half so that half start in the middle square and the others are around the circle with a ball.

HOW TO PLAY
The coach calls out a category at the start of each round. Players who start in the center square must check to an outside player and call out a name from the category the coach has chosen. For example the coach may say "Fruits". The center players must then run to the outside player and say the name of a fruit before the outside player will pass them the ball. The center players will receive the ball and play it back to the outside person. Center players must then run back through the square before checking to another outside player.

COACHING NOTES
+ Main coaching objectives – players check at an angle to 'open their body' to see the field.
+ Coaching tips – players need to cushion the ball when they receive it, but their first touch needs to be out from under them.
+ Adaptations – players can be split into thirds with one third in the middle and two thirds on the outsides

+ Outside players pass with their hands to check players.
+ Receiver should look over their shoulder before receiving the ball

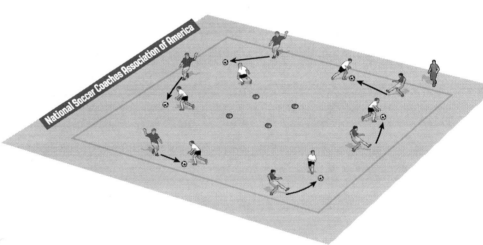

+ Center players check at an angle to receive the ball.
+ Coach can change the surface the receivers use to pass.

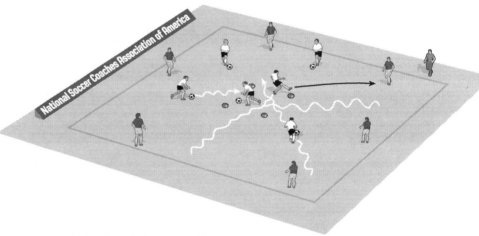

+ Players dribble through the center of the square.
+ Once through players pass the ball to an open player.

COCONUTS IN THE SKY

STAGES COVERED BY ACTIVITY
Stages 2 & 3 - 6-11 year old players

THEMES & COMPETENCIES
Theme:
+ Passing and receiving.

Competencies:
+ Passing over a short distance.
+ Receiving the ball with the feet.

WHY USE IT
This activity teaches players about passing accuracy and receiving

SET UP
25x20 grid with cones in the corners. 5 yard end zones are on each end line and there are 6 cones with a ball on top of each in the middle. These are the coconuts.

HOW TO PLAY
Players are split into 2 groups and they must stay in the end zones. The objective is to pass a ball to knock off the coconuts from the cones. Players in one end zone will receive balls that roll past the coconuts. The team that knocks off the most coconuts will win.

COACHING NOTES
+ Main coaching objectives – teach players to pass with greater accuracy and receive a ball to set up a pass.
+ Coaching tips – adjust the size of the grid to the players ability to pass over distance.
+ Adaptations – instead of keeping track of points, a team can win if they knock the last coconut off the cone.

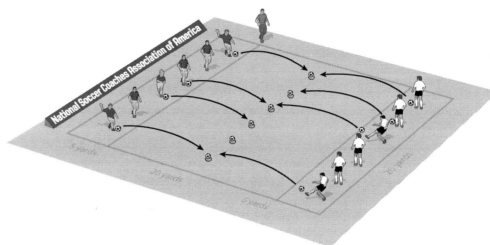

+ Players should take a setup touch before passing the ball.
+ Players may use different surfaces to receive the ball.

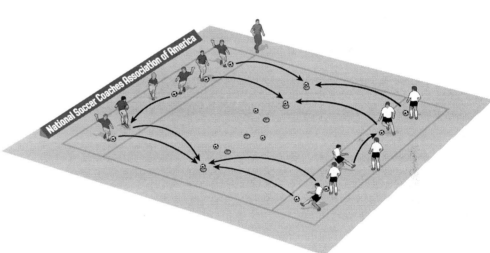

+ Receive with the knee over the ball and a cushioned touch
+ Players pass to teammates for a better chance at knocking off the coconut.

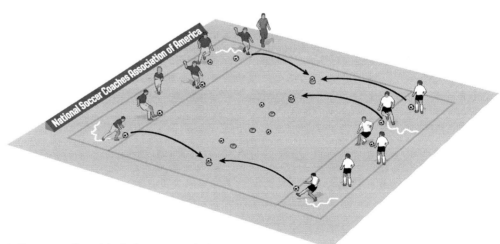

+ Players practice a feint before passing the ball.
+ Coach asks players to receive the ball and complete a move before passing.

STAGES COVERED BY ACTIVITY
Stages 2, 3 & 4 - 6-14 year old players

THEMES & COMPETENCIES
Theme:
+ Passing and receiving.

Competencies:
+ Passing over a short distance.
+ Receiving the ball with the feet.

WHY USE IT
Teach players to work in pairs using passing and moving with the ball.

SET UP
25x20 grid with cones in the corners. 12 gates of varying sizes made from two cones, are set up in the grid. Players are split into pairs and each pair has a ball.

HOW TO PLAY
Partners will first pass through a single gate to review passing technique. Pairs will then have one minute to pass through as many gates as they can. The coach should play several rounds to allow players to devise strategies that will allow them to improve their score.

COACHING NOTES
+ Main coaching objectives – players should improve passing accuracy, vision, and receiving the ball with their next movement in mind
+ Coaching tips – players should strike through the middle of the ball, use the metaphor of the ball is an "Oreo cookie" and players should hit the cream.
+ Adaptations – to increase difficulty one pair can act as bandits to try and steal the ball from other pairs

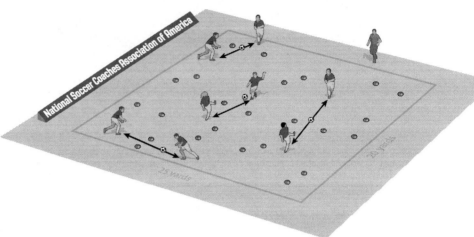

+ Partners pass between a gate - how many passes in a minute?
+ Coaches ask players to pass or receive with different surfaces of the foot.

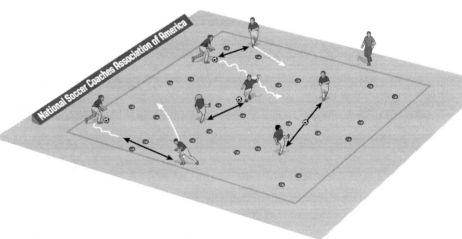

+ Players must pass and move to different gates.
+ Take a first touch in the direction of the next gate.
+ Think about the pace of the ball played to a partner.

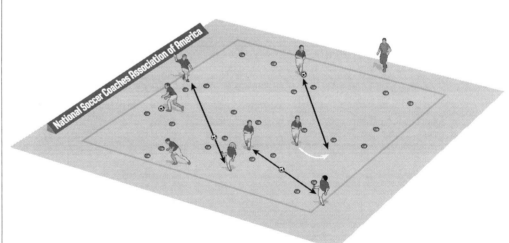

+ Players look to play the ball through more than one gate at a time.
+ Players think about short and long passes and the pace needed.

BOSS OF THE BALL PASSING

STAGES COVERED BY ACTIVITY
Stages 2, 3 & 4 - 6-14 year old players

THEMES & COMPETENCIES
Theme:
+ Passing and receiving.

Competencies:
+ Passing over a short distance.
+ Receiving the ball with the feet.

WHY USE IT
Players must work in groups and use their passing skills.

SET UP
25x20 yard grid with cones in the corners. 5 yard end zones are on each end line. The coach is in the middle of the touchline with all the balls. Players are split into 2 teams wearing different colored vests and lined up on either side of the coach.

HOW TO PLAY
The coach calls out a number and that number of players must enter the field of play. One team defends one end zone and the other team defends the other end zone. Teams get a point for each time they can complete a pass to someone in the opposition's end zone.

COACHING NOTES
+ Main coaching objectives – players must work together using their passing accuracy and timing of their runs.
+ Coaching tips – instead of stopping play, coaches can use the time that players are waiting in line to give instructions
+ Adaptations – if there are more than 4 players waiting in a line look to create a second grid for play

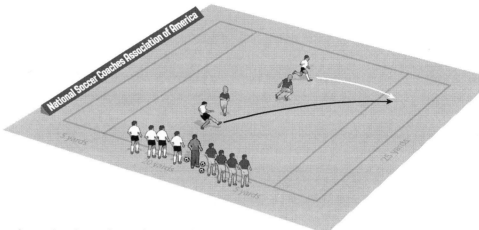

+ Supporting players change their pace in order to lose defenders.
+ Player on the ball must use the proper weight of pass.

+ First touch to go forward.
+ It is important to engage a defender to set up a pass.

+ Points awarded if players receive the ball as they are running into the end zone.
+ Discuss the importance of the timing of runs.

CAPTURE THE BALL

STAGES COVERED BY ACTIVITY
Stages 2, 3 & 4 - 6-14 year old players

THEMES & COMPETENCIES
Theme:
+ Passing and receiving.

Competencies:
+ Passing over a short distance.
+ Receiving the ball with the feet.

WHY USE IT
Players must use their passing skills in small groups and with opposition.

SET UP
25x20 grid with cones in the corners. 6 balls are placed on top of cones 5 yards off each end line. Players are split into teams of 4 and each team is in a different colored vest. The coach is in the middle of the touchline with extra soccer balls.

HOW TO PLAY
2 teams will play 3 minute games. The coach will play balls in to restart the activity. Teams must try to pass a ball and knock one of the balls off the cones. If they are successful, then they move the ball and the cone to their side of the field and set it up there. The winner at the end of 3 minutes is the team with the most balls set up on their side.

COACHING NOTES
+ Main coaching objectives – players must work together and use their passing accuracy
+ Coaching tips – make sure to play balls into players that may not be as active in order to include them
+ Adaptations – use multiple balls at a time if any players are inactive

+ Player's first touch should take them away from pressure.
+ Player's body position should allow them to see the field.

+ Players should look to communicate and support their teammates.
+ Players are allowed to move behind the balls to support the pass.

+ Introducing multiple balls allows more players to be involved.
+ Players should look to use long and short passes.

ICE MONSTER

STAGES COVERED BY ACTIVITY
Stages 2 - 6-8 year old players

THEMES & COMPETENCIES
Theme:
+ Dribbling and turns.
+ Attacking as an individual.
+ Defending as an individual.

Competencies:
+ Dribbling basics.
+ Turning basics.
+ Feints and dribble.
+ Beating an opponent.
+ Escaping an opponent.

WHY USE IT
This is a great game to introduce the idea of patience when defending and not diving in to win a ball.

SET UP
Create a 20x20 grid. 8 players each have a ball and are dribbling. 4 players (Ice Monsters), are each holding a colored vest. Eight gates of varying sizes are positioned in the grid.

HOW TO PLAY
Players are on a frozen island. Players with a ball dribble around for 1-2 minutes to see how many gates (heaters) they can get through. The 4 Ice Monsters are trying to freeze players by tapping the ball of a dribbler with their foot. If a dribbler's ball is tapped by an Ice Monster they must freeze in place. Players are unfrozen when another dribbler comes up to them and does 4 toe touches on the ball to heat them up. Switch Ice Monsters every 1-2 minutes.

COACHING NOTES
+ Main coaching objectives – defenders must maintain control of their body and not just kick the ball away
+ Coaching tips – adjust the gate size to challenge the players
+ Adaptations – Ice Monsters hold the vest and try to win the ball back. If they are successful they drop the vest and the player who lost the ball becomes the Ice Monster.

+ Ice Monsters must stay low and keep their feet moving in order to tap the ball away

+ Ice Monsters can work together to corner a player

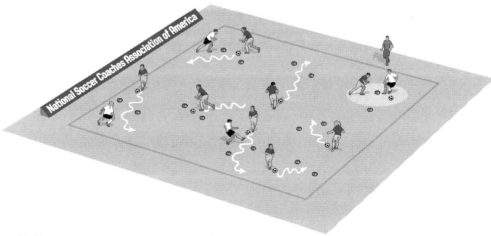

+ Ice Monsters can win the ball and switch roles

MINUTE TO WIN IT

STAGES COVERED BY ACTIVITY
Stages 2, 3 & 4- 6-14 year old players

THEMES & COMPETENCIES
Theme:
+ Dribbling and turns.
+ Attacking as an individual.
+ Defending as an individual.

Competencies:
+ Dribbling basics.
+ Turning basics.
+ Feints and dribble.
+ Beating an opponent.
+ Escaping an opponent.

WHY USE IT
This activity focuses on players speed and angle of approach when defending.

SET UP
Create a 20x20 grid. Players are in lines of 3-4 players in the corners of the area. There is a 2 yard gate goal in each corner of the field.

HOW TO PLAY
The first person in line plays a ball across the area on the diagonal to line 3 and then runs to defend. If the player from line 3 can dribble through the 'gate' defended by the player from line 1, he/she earns a point. If the defender from line 1 can win possession, he/she has 2 options:
1. Attempt to play back to his/her team for a point
2. Play it through the gate of line 3 for 2 points.
Once the game has finished, the first player from line 2 plays the ball across to line 4 for a similar game. Play for 2 minutes and then switch roles.

COACHING NOTES
+ Main coaching objectives – defenders angle of approach to force the attacker away from goal; defenders speed of approach
+ Coaching tips – create teaching moments and talk to players as they are waiting in line to allow for more repetitions
+ Adaptations – have more than one group play at the same time; or have a trigger word to stop play if players are static and not attacking the goal.

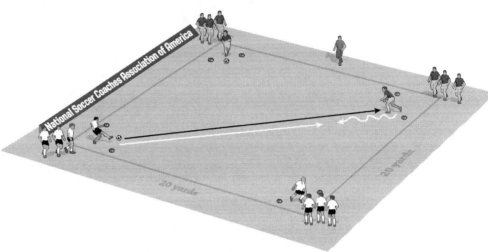

+ The defender sprints to the attacker to apply pressure.
+ Slow down and take smaller steps as the defender gets close to the attacker.

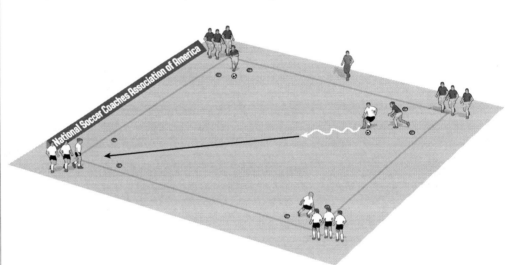

+ The defender needs to read when the ball comes off the attacker's foot, so that they can win it.
+ If the defender wins the ball, he/she should look to see if they can penetrate to goal or play back to a teammate.

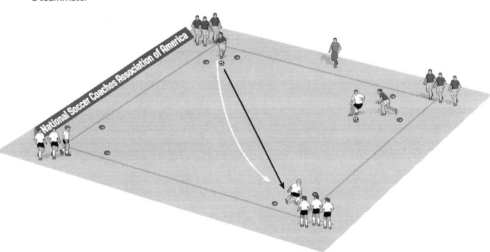

+ As two players are working, a second group can start to play to keep the game active.

ICE CREAM SCOOP CHALLENGE

STAGES COVERED BY ACTIVITY
Stages 2, 3 & 4 - 6-14 year old players

THEMES & COMPETENCIES
Theme:
+ Dribbling and turns.
+ Attacking as an individual.
+ Defending as an individual.

Competencies:
+ Dribbling basics.
+ Turning basics.
+ Feints and dribble.
+ Beating an opponent.
+ Escaping an opponent.

WHY USE IT
This 1v1 game allows players to work on their defensive approach and stance. In addition this allows attacking players to practice moves to beat a defender.

SET UP
Create 2 - 10x15 yard areas. Place a cone with a ball on top 2 yards off the end line of each grid. The coach will stand in the coaching channel between the two grids. Divide players into 4 groups with 2 groups starting on opposite end lines.

HOW TO PLAY
One side of the area starts attacking. The coach plays a ball into the attacking player. The attacking player attempts to beat the defender and pass the ball to knock the ice cream off the cone. If the defending player wins the ball they can try to knock the ice cream off the other cone.

COACHING NOTES
+ Main coaching objectives – can players recognize when to slow down and keep their body under control in order to keep the attacker in front of them.
+ Coaching tips – try to have lines be uneven so as to avoid players going against the same teammate.
+ Adaptations – this activity can build to 2v1 or 2v2.

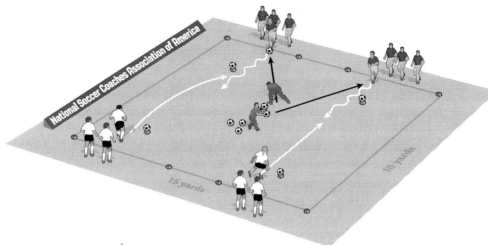

+ Defender sprints to the attacker to apply pressure.
+ Defender slows down to take smaller steps as they get closer.

+ Players should keep feet moving.
+ Players should angle their body and attempt to keep the attacking player in front.

+ When the defender wins the ball, quickly transition to attack.

2V2 TRANSITION TO GOAL KEEPER

STAGES COVERED BY ACTIVITY
Stages 2, 3 & 4 - 6-14 year old players

THEMES & COMPETENCIES
Theme:
+ Dribbling and turns.
+ Attacking as an individual.
+ Defending as an individual.
+ Passing and receiving.

Competencies:
+ Dribbling basics.
+ Turning basics.
+ Feints and dribble.
+ Beating an opponent.
+ Escaping an opponent.
+ Passing over a short distance.
+ Receiving the ball with the feet.

WHY USE IT
This is a fun transition game and allows players to work on their individual defending and communication with a partner.

SET UP
Create several 10x20 grids with a small goal on each end line. This will allow for multiple groups to play at the same time. Players will be split into teams of 2.

HOW TO PLAY
The team without the ball will play with 1 player on the field as a defender and the other player is restricted to the area in front of the goal to act as a keeper. If the defender wins the ball, she must play the ball back to the keeper, to start the attack. The team that lost possession will then have one player assume the role of the goalkeeper and the other a defender.

COACHING NOTES
+ Main coaching objectives – players should think about their defensive body position and approach to the ball
+ Coaching tips – switch teams every few games to allow players to work with other teammates
+ Adaptations – players do not need to play the ball back to the keeper before starting the attack to allow for a quicker transition from defense to attack

+ Pressure - Defender makes an angled run attempting to cut off the pass to the other attacker

+ Defender should stay low and keep their feet moving to force the attacker to the side line

+ If the defender sees an opportunity to win the ball they should do so and play to their keeper to transition to attack.

3V3 CHANGE GAME

STAGES COVERED BY ACTIVITY
Stages 2, 3 & 4 - 6-14 year old players

THEMES & COMPETENCIES
Theme:
+ Dribbling and turns.
+ Attacking as an individual.
+ Defending as an individual.
+ Passing and receiving.

Competencies:
+ Dribbling basics.
+ Turning basics.
+ Feints and dribble.
+ Beating an opponent.
+ Escaping an opponent.
+ Passing over a short distance.
+ Receiving the ball with the feet.

WHY USE IT
This game has players working in small groups with an emphasis on communication and putting pressure on the ball.

SET UP
20x25 yard grid divided into 3 zones. Middle zone is 15 yards long and end zones are 5 yards deep. A large goal created from flags on each end line. 4 teams of 3 players wearing a different colored vest.

HOW TO PLAY
2 teams play 3v3 in the middle area. The remaining teams act as the goalkeepers. The 3 players on those teams must hold hands as they move around the goal. When the coach says the word "Alakazam" the two teams in the middle switch with the two teams acting as goalkeepers.

COACHING NOTES
+ Main coaching objectives – team communication and pressure on the ball.
+ Coaching tips – make the goals big enough so that keepers must move to defend them and work together
+ Adaptations – Instead of calling "Alakazam" the coach can call out the two colors that will play each other, so that teams can play a new opponent.

+ Teams must communicate and to decide who puts pressure on the ball.

+ When the attack passes the ball defenders must adjust to keep players in front of them.

+ Coach calls "Alakazam" teams leave ball and switch roles.

HOW TO FEED YOUR DRAGON

STAGES COVERED BY ACTIVITY
Stages 1 & 2 - 3-8 year old players

THEMES & COMPETENCIES
Theme:
+ Dribbling and turns.
+ Attacking as an individual.
+ Defending as an individual.

Competencies:
+ Dribbling basics.
+ Turning basics.
+ Feints and dribble.
+ Beating an opponent.
+ Escaping an opponent.

WHY USE IT
A simple game incorporating agility with goal scoring with the inside of the foot.

SET UP
25x25yd area. 3 small goals are set up in the middle of 3 sidelines. Balls are placed in the middle of the 4th sideline - inside a semi circle created with cones. Make sure there is at least 1 ball per player. A minimum of 10 gates (varying distances apart) are spread throughout the grid.

HOW TO PLAY
3 teams each stand next to a goal. The goal represents the team's 'Pet Dragon' and the balls are food for the dragon. When the coach says "GO" the 1st person in each line moves through 3 sets of gates to 'power up'. The players will then get a ball from the pile. The player is allowed to take 1 piece of food/ball and dribble it back near their goal before passing it into the dragon's mouth/goal. Once the first person has gone the next person in line will repeat the activity. Time teams and/or see which team feed the dragon the most.

COACHING NOTES
+ Main coaching objectives – warm players up with various movements; accuracy of finishing with inside of foot
+ Coaching tips – to get players finishing from farther away set up a shooting zone in front of the goal
+ Adaptations – players dribble back through 3 gates before shooting.

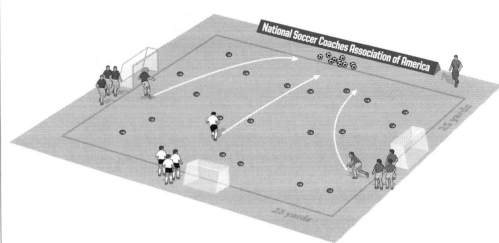

+ Coach assigns a different movement for each round of the game (jogging, skipping, carioca etc)
+ Players must move through three gates before getting a ball

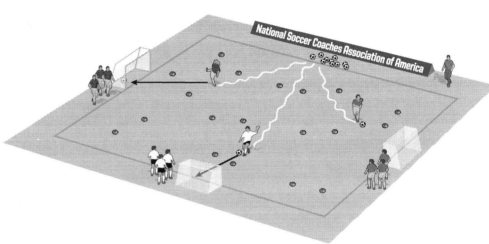

+ Players must get the ball and then dribble back to their goal to shoot
+ Plant foot needs to point towards the goal when finishing

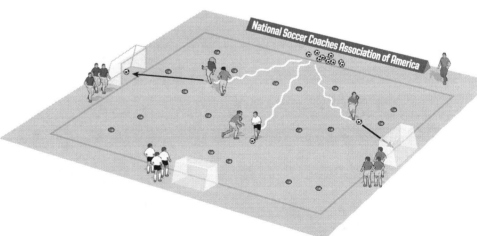

+ The coach can assign two players as bandits who act as passive defenders.
+ When finishing players must keep their head down and strike through the middle of the ball

POPCORN

STAGES COVERED BY ACTIVITY
Stages 1 & 2 - 3-8 year old players

THEMES & COMPETENCIES
Theme:
+ Dribbling and turns.
+ Attacking as an individual.
+ Defending as an individual.
+ Passing and receiving.

Competencies:
+ Dribbling basics.
+ Turning basics.
+ Feints and dribble.
+ Beating an opponent.
+ Escaping an opponent.
+ Passing and receiving.

WHY USE IT
Players learn how to shoot off the dribble using their instep.

SET UP
30x20yd area. 2 goals. In the middle there is zone the width of the space and 8-10 yards long. 2 teams wearing a colored vest. Every player starts with a ball in the middle zone. Players assigned a number 1-6. Goalkeepers in each net.

HOW TO PLAY
Story: Players are each an individual piece of corn and the middle zone is the popcorn pot. Teams are assigned to a goal that they will try to score in. Players dribble in the middle zone avoiding each other and heating up in the pot. The coach calls a number and players from each team must "pop" out of the pot (by dribbling) and then shoot on their goal. Coaches can see who can score the most goals in two minutes.

COACHING NOTES
+ Main coaching objectives – player's shooting technique: toe down, ankle locked, knee over the ball and striking with their laces
+ Coaching tips – use parent volunteers to help collect soccer balls
+ Adaptations – coach calls out a color and a number, so that the player whose color is called is attacking their goal and the player with the same number on the other team must try to defend them.

+ Players dribble around the middle zone avoiding other players and working on different moves until their number is called.

+ When a player hears their number, they should make a clean move to turn to goal
+ Make sure that players have the ball under their knee or a little in front when shooting

+ Make sure players are striking the ball with their laces and keeping their head down

1V1 BOX COMPETITION

STAGES COVERED BY ACTIVITY
Stages 1 & 2 - 3-8 year old players

THEMES & COMPETENCIES
Theme:
+ Dribbling and turns.
+ Attacking as an individual.
+ Defending as an individual.

Competencies:
+ Dribbling basics.
+ Turning basics.
+ Feints and dribble.
+ Beating an opponent.
+ Escaping an opponent.
+ Shooting technique.

WHY USE IT
This activity allows for players to gain confidence executing a move to beat a defender to set up a shot.

SET UP
2 fields are set up side by side. A large goal is placed in each field. Each field is 30x15 with a 8x8 yard box about 15 yards from the goal. Players are split into teams and each team is positioned behind a cone 5 yards behind the grid.

HOW TO PLAY
The first person in each line must dribble up to the grid and perform a move to beat a defender. The player will then look to dribble and score at the edge of the grid. The coach will tell the teams that they have two minutes to see how many goals they can score. In the second phase a defender is added in each grid.

COACHING NOTES
+ Main coaching objectives – increase comfort attacking 1v1 and shooting on goal
+ Coaching tips – remind players of the timing of their move versus the defender and to have a prep touch that gets their body facing the goal when shooting.
+ Adaptations – the distance of the grid from the goal can be adjusted to make it harder or easier to score.

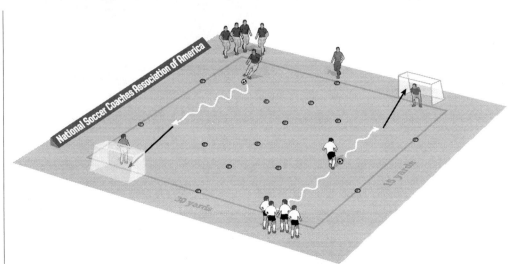

+ Players must keep the ball close to them when performing the move before shooting.

+ The player must now try to beat the defender in the box before shooting.
+ Players need to focus on the timing of the move to beat the defender.

+ If the defender wins the ball they can dribble out of the grid for a point

STAR WARS 3V1

STAGES COVERED BY ACTIVITY
Stages 2, 3 & 4 - 6-14 year old players

THEMES & COMPETENCIES
Theme:
+ Dribbling and turns.
+ Attacking as an individual.
+ Defending as an individual.
+ Passing and receiving.

Competencies:
+ Dribbling basics.
+ Turning basics.
+ Feints and dribble.
+ Beating an opponent.
+ Escaping an opponent.
+ Passing and receiving.

WHY USE IT
Players must work together to create scoring chances in the box.

SET UP
20x35 yard area. Players are split into 2 teams. The attacking team is 5 yards from the top of the box in teams of 3. The defending team forms a line on the end line. Add a goalkeeper. Coach is positioned near the attackers with the soccer balls.

HOW TO PLAY
The coach plays a ball into one of the players at the top of the box. As the coach plays the ball the first person in the defending line will run out to defend 3v1. The attacking team works together to try and score in the big goal.

COACHING NOTES
+ Main coaching objectives – players body position when receiving; 1st touch is out from under them to set up a quick shot
+ Coaching tips – vary which line the ball is served into to involve more players
+ Adaptations – increase the difficult by allowing another defender to enter once the attacker makes the first pass.

+ First player to receive the ball should look to see if they can shoot immediately.
+ If the defender closes the shot, can the player pass to an open teammate?

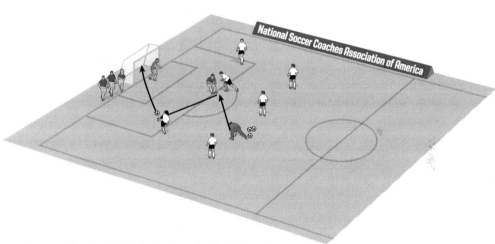

+ Players must position their body to receive the ball so that they are facing the goal.
+ A player's first touch should be out from underneath them to allow for them to step and shoot.

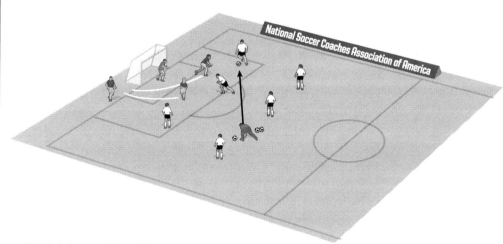

+ Remind players to have their head over the ball when shooting and avoid leaning back
+ A second defender can join in after the first pass is made.

TRIANGLE GOAL GAME

STAGES COVERED BY ACTIVITY
Stages 2, 3 & 4 - 6-14 year old players

THEMES & COMPETENCIES
Theme:
+ Attacking as an individual.
+ Passing and receiving.

Competencies:
+ Beating an opponent.
+ Escaping an opponent.
+ Passing and receiving.

WHY USE IT
This game creates continuous shooting opportunities and allows teams to work together to create shooting angles.

SET UP
35x35 yard grid marked by cones in the corner. A triangle goal is in the middle of the grid with flags 8 feet apart. Players are split into two teams of 5 and there are two goalkeepers defending the three goals created by the triangle. (Parents may also be used as goalkeepers if needed.) The coach is positioned in one corner with all the soccer balls.

HOW TO PLAY
The coach plays a ball into one of the teams. The teams can shoot through any side of the triangle goal. Goal is worth 1 point. The ball remains in play once it goes through the triangle and it is available for whichever team wins it. If a keeper saves the ball, they distribute it to the coach. The coach can keep track of goals scored and saves made to create a competition between the two teams and the keepers.

COACHING NOTES
+ Main coaching objectives – 1st touch to set up a shot; movement from players to create scoring chances.
+ Coaching tips – create a 5 yard area out from the goal, so that players are not shooting too close to the keepers.
+ Adaptations – to create more scoring chances add 1-2 neutral players.

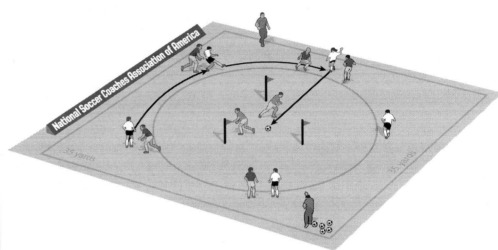

+ Players must pass the ball to find an open shooting angle.
+ The toe should be down, ankle locked and knee over the ball when striking it with the laces.

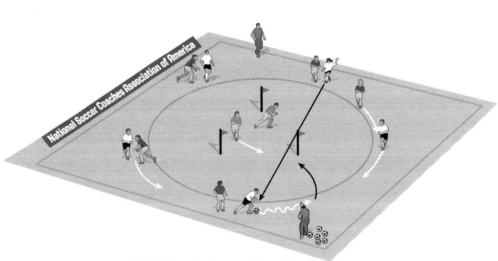

+ The player receiving the ball from the shot needs to cushion the ball.
+ Players without the ball should look to move to support the player on the ball

+ If a keeper makes a save they should throw the ball to the coach

STAGE 3 - ADOLESCENCE/EARLY PUBERTY (9-11 YEARS OLD)

This is the beginning of pre-adolescence. Children begin to 'spread out' as their rate of development accelerates. Girls in particular start to physically mature quicker than boys and this growth surge can lead to awkward performance, particularly on tasks requiring fine motor movements. As friendships are developing and players are becoming more reliant on their peers it is important for team selection to be handled sensitively. The reason why so many athletes plateau during the later stages of their careers is primarily because of an over-emphasis on competition instead of training during this important period in their development.

DEVELOPMENT FOCUS

- This is a crucial time for developing advanced competency in basic techniques and this platform allows for the introduction of more advanced skills.
- Some basic tactical appreciation can also be introduced.
- Commence aerobic capacity training at stage 3, prior to the adolescent growth spurt, also known as Peak Height Velocity
- Aerobic power should be introduced progressively after growth rate decelerates.
- It is also very important that children are encouraged to take part in unstructured play and other sport participation is encouraged.

KEY DEVELOPMENT POINTS FOR CHILDREN IN STAGE 3		
Physically	**Psychological/Social**	**Cognitive/Mental**
1. Heart size is increasing in relation to body size.	1. Individual need for attention and 'showmanship' is common.	1. Attention span continues to increase.
2. The players ability to perform anaerobically (high intensity and short duration movements) is limited due to slow development of anaerobic energy system.	2. Self confidence and self awareness is developing through peer group experiences.	2. Players still prefer to learn by doing – players can become impatient quickly.
3. The players aerobic system (activities lasting for durations of 30 seconds plus) is not as efficient as older players.	3. Structured environments provide comfort.	3. Players learn by repetition.
4. Large muscle groups are more defined than small muscle groups.	4. Players generally like consistency in approach and application of rules, etc.	4. A predominant learning style begins to surface – most children learn by doing
5. Extreme heat and cold affects players rapidly.		5. Language is not fully developed so players find it hard to articulate fully.
6. Players develop balance due to changes in the functionality of the inner ear.		
7. Developments in the nervous system facilitate the development of strength.		
8. Onset of puberty in females results in breast and hip-width development impeding performance and fall behind late developers.		
9. Early developing males are bigger and stronger than late developers and often experience success.		

DEVELOPMENT CHARACTERISTICS TRANSLATED TO COACHING PLAYERS IN STAGE 3

With appropriate coaching and focus on fundamental movement and basic soccer skills at Stage 1 and Stage 2, the performance of players at Stage 3 start to resemble more traditional soccer that we witness adults and older youth play. A player in possession will be thinking of passing to a team mate and will understand the need to support in attack and defense. Players will have greater awareness for the team, allowing coaches to develop simple tactics involving small groups and units. However, coaches must not abandon individual skill development and this focus must continue to take precedent over team tactics.

TRANSLATED TO PLAYER DEVELOPMENT THIS MEANS

1. Players can perform lower intensity activity for at least an hour.

2. Speed and endurance activities should be included to train and enhance the development of the energy systems.

3. Girls – be conscious that girls going through puberty are more susceptible to drop out so be patient and provide plenty of encouragement.

4. Boys – early developers will dominate other players by virtue of their size and speed. Ensure that evaluations are based on several factors including execution of technique and understanding the game.

5. Players at this stage in their development cannot maintain exercise intensities or durations that players in the next stage can.

6. Technical development must form a large focus of training and players should be encouraged to practice at home informally and skills such as juggling and 'freestyle' moves should be encouraged.

7. Warm-up activities are important to raise body temperature and heart rate.

8. Players must be encouraged to drink plenty of fluids prior to practices/games and they must replenish lost fluids during and after activity.

9. Correct technique must be emphasized to complement the development of neural pathways.

10. Sessions should be progressed into small sided games/activities – 2 v 1 and 3 v 2 with a neutral player playing for the team in possession is an excellent ways to introduce introductory tactics.

11. Sessions can follow a theme but activities should be changed regularly to maintain interest.

12. Encourage and reward creativity in practice and games.

13. Different learning styles must be accommodated, so different coaching methodologies should be employed.

14. Praise and reward effort and create many opportunities for success.

15. Positive coaching focusing on strengths promotes confidence and self esteem.

16. Set goals and high expectations for all players.

17. Continue to encourage players to engage in unstructured physical play

18. Players should be working on flexibility, speed, endurance and strength. Strength activities should be using their own body weight, Swiss Balls and Medicine Balls.

4 CORNER GAME

STAGES COVERED BY ACTIVITY

Stages 3, 4 & 5 - 9-18 year old players

THEMES & COMPETENCIES

Theme:
+ Passing combinations
+ Attacking transition.
+ Defending in pairs and groups.

Competencies:
+ Short passing along the ground (5-15 yards).
+ Receiving using the feet.
+ Mobility on and off the ball.
+ Attacking and defending as an individual.
+ Attacking and defending in pairs and small groups.
+ Attacking support.

WHY USE IT

This activity helps develop a rhythm in possession and combination play. Players also appreciate that space gets less as play progresses forward.

SET UP

25x25 yard square. Play 3v3 in the area for possession with each team having two players in a corner zone across from each other on the diagonal to make a 5v5.

HOW TO PLAY

In possession teams look to use the corner players to support the play. If the ball can be moved from one corner to the other the team scores a point and the play is continued without stoppage. When a successful pass is made to the corner player, the passer switches places as the game continues to flow.

COACHING NOTES

+ Coaching objectives – to improve the players recognition of support in possession.
+ Coaching tip – work the activity for short periods with the ball always in play.
+ Adaptations – increase challenge with touch restrictions and allow the target players to enter the field.

+ Blue target passes to a well-marked team mate who cannot turn.
+ The target moves in support to receive the ball back.
+ The pass is played to an open support player.

+ A pass to a target scores a point.
+ The target immediately begins play with a dribble.
+ The passer moves into the corner.

+ The blue team completes two passes to score.
+ Target plays a quick give and go.
+ Passing sequence allows the target to get into space.

COCONUTS

STAGES COVERED BY ACTIVITY

Stages 2 & 3 - 6-11 year old players.

THEMES & COMPETENCIES

Theme:
+ Passing combinations.
+ Attacking transition.
+ Defending in pairs and groups.

Competencies:
+ Short passing along the ground (5-15 yards).
+ Receiving using the feet.
+ Mobility on and off the ball.
+ Attacking and defending as an individual.
+ Attacking and defending in pairs and small groups.
+ Attacking support.

WHY USE IT

This activity has a lot of technical challenges and also introduces the idea of switching the point of attack and moving off the ball into advanced positions.

SET UP

30x25 yard area. Set up inside the playing space 3 balls on top of cones at both sides of the area to create targets. The targets are 5 yards from each end line.

HOW TO PLAY

The object of the game is to pass or dribble the game ball into a target and dislodge the target ball. If a score is achieved the target is reset and play continues. Players are encouraged to use the playing space behind the targets when on attack.

COACHING NOTES

+ Coaching objectives – to encourage players to play forward or to switch play.
+ Coaching tip – remind players on the available space vertically and horizontally.
+ Adaptations – observe the offside rule. Players cannot go behind targets until the ball is played.

+ The player in possession identifies a clear passing channel between two opponents and has a clear sight of the target.
+ An accurate and weighted inside of the foot pass is used to try to score.

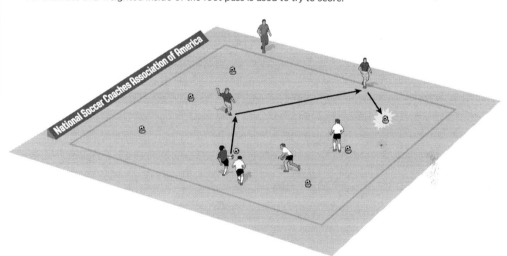

+ The defending team is effective in denying a clear channel to the targets.
+ The player in possession elects to pass the ball on and initiate a quick switch of the play.
+ The player on the far side receives the ball with time to pass at, or dribble over, or into the target.

+ The defending team is effective in denying a clear channel to the targets and has the far side player marked.
+ As the play is switched the far side player moves into a position behind the target.
+ If the shot at the target misses, the far side player is in position to collect the ball and keep the attack alive.

COMBINATION WARM-UP

STAGES COVERED BY ACTIVITY

Stages 3, 4 & 5 - 9-18 year old players

THEMES & COMPETENCIES

Theme:
+ Passing combinations

Competencies:
+ Short passing along the ground (5-15 yards).
+ Receiving using the feet.
+ Mobility on and off the ball.

WHY USE IT

As a warm up to get players passing and moving in combinations of 3 players.

SET UP

Circle approximately 20 yard diameter. 6 players form a circle and the other 6 players get into pairs with a ball between them.

HOW TO PLAY

The pairs in the middle of the circle pass back and forth and every few passes look to combine with a peripheral support player. The peripheral player returns a pass to the other partner. The partners pass back and forth before one passes to an outside player who then plays the ball back to the other partner.

COACHING NOTES

+ Coaching objectives – to activate the players physically and mentally.
+ Coaching tip – have players switch in and out on the fly rather than stop the action.
+ Adaptations – include a defender in the middle to challenge the pairs awareness.

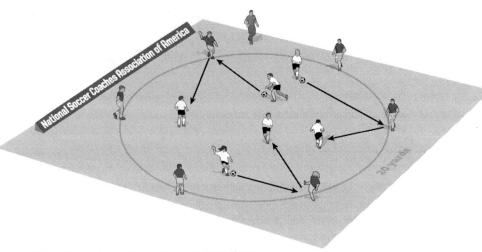

+ Pairs in the circle combine with a peripheral player.
+ Peripheral player passes back to other partner.
+ The outside player must be alert.

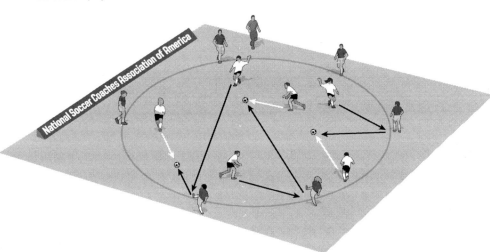

+ Ball is played to peripheral player.
+ The other center player moves short or long.
+ Peripheral player must be aware of movement towards or away from him/her.

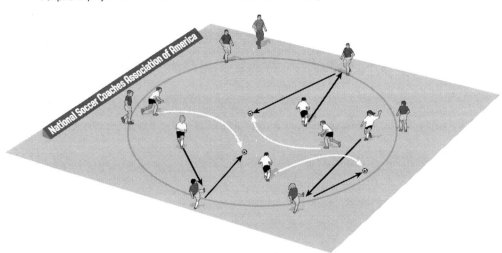

+ The inside receiver makes a shaped run to an open space.
+ Peripheral player plays a pass to space.

STAGES COVERED BY ACTIVITY

Stages 3, 4 & 5 - 9-18 year old players

THEMES & COMPETENCIES

Theme:
+ Passing combinations
+ Attacking transition.
+ Defending in pairs and groups.

Competencies:
+ Short passing along the ground (5-15 yards).
+ Receiving using the feet.
+ Mobility on and off the ball.
+ Attacking and defending as an individual.
+ Attacking and defending in pairs and small groups.
+ Attacking support.

WHY USE IT

This activity helps players develop a rhythm and purpose in possession.

SET UP

30x30 yard square. Play is 3v3 in the area with a target player on two sides for each team (5v5). The target players are on opposite sides of the square.

HOW TO PLAY

Each team seeks to maintain possession using their target players. The objective is to move across the square by combining passes and avoiding turning the ball over to the other team.

COACHING NOTES

+ Coaching objectives – to encourage players to be positive in possession.
+ Coaching tip – observe the supporting movements of the target players.
+ Adaptations – once a pass is made to the target, the passer can switch positions with the target player on the fly.

+ Blue team combined effectively from one target to the other.
+ Target players move along the line to receive the final pass.

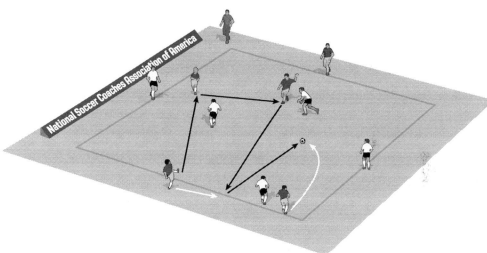

+ The white team defends well.
+ The target player moves well in support of the ball.
+ The target player is involved multiple times.

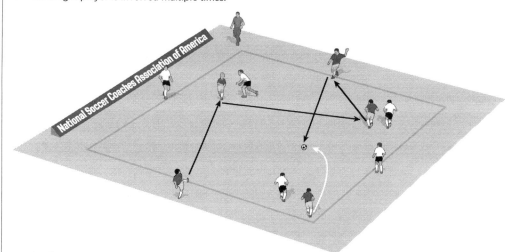

+ Off the ball an inside player anticipates and moves to receive.
+ An immediate pass from the second target player maintains possession.

STAGES COVERED BY ACTIVITY

Stages 3, 4 & 5 - 9-18 year old players

THEMES & COMPETENCIES

Theme:
+ Passing combinations.
+ Attacking transition.
+ Defending in pairs and groups.
+ Shooting

Competencies:
+ Short passing along the ground (5-15 yards).
+ Receiving using the feet.
+ Mobility on and off the ball.
+ Attacking and defending as an individual.
+ Attacking and defending in pairs and small groups.
+ Attacking support.
+ Shooting technique

WHY USE IT

The activity encourages speed of play and positive transitions to attack.

SET UP

35x25 yard field with 5 yard end zones and small goals. Play is 4v4.

HOW TO PLAY

The game commences with the coach passing to one of the teams of 4. The defending team must drop one player back into the end zone, to leave 3 defenders against 4 attackers. When the ball is turned over, the team losing possession must drop a player into the defensive zone and the attacking team can attack at full strength – 4v3.

COACHING NOTES

+ Coaching objectives – to get players to play fast and positive in attacking transition.
+ Coaching tip – have a good supply of balls so play is continuous and fast paced.
+ Adaptations – allow the attacking team to penetrate the end zone on the dribble.

+ The player with the ball commits the opponent on the dribble.
+ The other 3 attacking players move wide and with good movement get open.
+ 4 white players establish a shape to stretch the 3 blue players.

+ The blue team's strike at goal is saved.
+ White team quickly transition with an outlet pass.
+ Simultaneously, one of the blue players immediately recovers to the goal.

+ The white team breaks down the well-organized defense.
+ A give and go eliminates a blue opponent allowing the white player to get into the space behind.

FAST BREAK GAME

STAGES COVERED BY ACTIVITY
Stages 3, 4 & 5 - 9-18 year old players

THEMES & COMPETENCIES
Theme:
+ Passing combinations
+ Attacking transition.
+ Defending in pairs and groups.
+ Shooting

Competencies:
+ Short passing along the ground (5-15 yards).
+ Receiving using the feet.
+ Mobility on and off the ball.
+ Attacking and defending as an individual.
+ Attacking and defending in pairs and small groups.
+ Attacking support.
+ Shooting technique

WHY USE IT
To encourage players to attack the goal numbers up with speed.

SET UP
35x25 yard space. 14 players split into 2 teams. 2 goals. A goalkeeper in each end. Start with 3 blues and a goalkeeper vs 2 whites and a goalkeeper - with extra players for both teams on the side of the field.

HOW TO PLAY
Commence the game with the coach playing a pass to blues. Blues attack the white's goal. When a goal is scored or the defending team wins possession (turnover) the team winning possession add an extra attacker and the opponent drops a player to create a 3v2 overload in the other direction.

COACHING NOTES
+ Coaching objectives – to have players play with positivity and creativity when attacking the goal.
+ Coaching tip – really focus on the moment of transition to attack and encourage speed of play.
+ Adaptations – increase the field size and the playing numbers for added complexity.

+ Start with 3v2.
+ Attacking 3 players commit the opposing defenders.

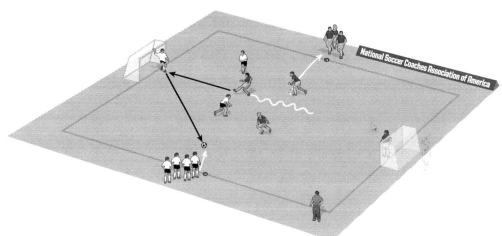

+ Goalkeeper immediately sends the ball to the next white player 'on deck'.
+ During a turnover, an attacker must leave the field.

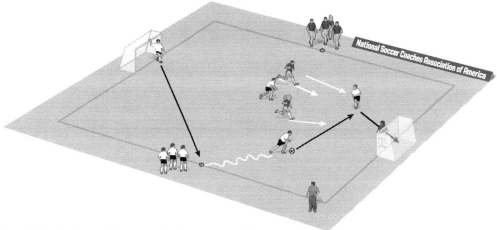

+ 2 defenders immediately transition into open attacking spaces
+ 3v2 the other way.

TRIANGLE TECHNICAL WARM UP

STAGES COVERED BY ACTIVITY
Stages 3, 4 & 5 - 9-18 year old players

THEMES & COMPETENCIES
Theme:
+ Passing combinations

Competencies:
+ Short passing along the ground (5-15 yards).
+ Receiving using the feet.
+ Mobility on and off the ball.
+ Attacking support.

WHY USE IT
To physically activate players in a technical pattern warm up, focussing on passing, receiving and movement with the ball.

SET UP
3 cones, 10-15 yards apart, make an equilateral triangle. At 2 of the cones there is a player and at one cone there are 2 players. Play commences from the cone with 2 players.

HOW TO PLAY
The warm up activity has a series of prescribed progressions of passing and movement. To begin, players pass to the outside of the triangle in a clockwise direction. The pass should be firm and along the ground. Once a rhythm has been established the coach can introduce passing combinations such as a give and go or overlap.

COACHING NOTES
+ Coaching objectives – to get the players passing and moving with purpose.
+ Coaching tip – encourage/demand technical sharpness as the activity is unopposed.
+ Adaptations – develop into 1 or 2 touches, and have groups of 4 compete against time.

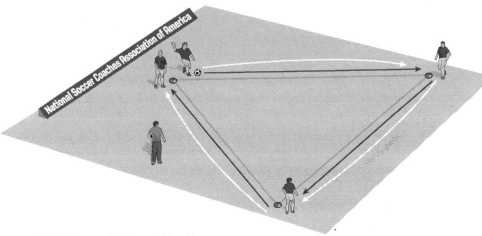

+ The ball is passed to the outside of the cone.
+ The passer then follows their pass.
+ The receiver passes the ball on to the next player.

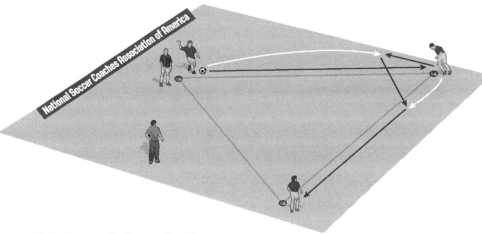

+ The ball is passed to the outside of the cone.
+ The receiver passes the ball back.
+ A give and go is completed around the cone.

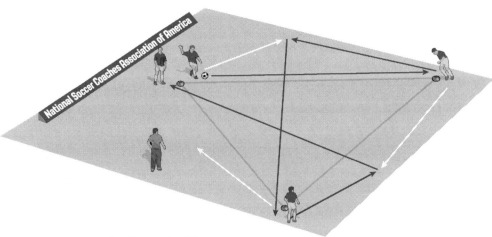

+ The ball is passed to the outside of the cone.
+ The receiver passes the ball back.
+ The ball is passed across the triangle.

SUBS UP

STAGES COVERED BY ACTIVITY
Stages 3, 4 & 5 - 9-18 year old players

THEMES & COMPETENCIES
Theme:
+ Passing combinations
+ Attacking transition.
+ Defending in pairs and groups.
+ Shooting

Competencies:
+ Short passing along the ground (5-15 yards).
+ Receiving using the feet.
+ Mobility on and off the ball.
+ Attacking and defending as an individual.
+ Attacking and defending in pairs and small groups.
+ Attacking support.
+ Shooting technique

WHY USE IT
To encourage players to react quickly to transition moments of the game.

SET UP
25x20 yard area with a goal at each end. Players are split into 2 teams with a goalkeeper for each team. Play 3v3 with extra players for both teams on the side of the field.

HOW TO PLAY
Every time the ball goes out of play the coach serves in another ball. After a number of repetitions the coach calls "subs up" and all players must exchange with teammates. The players and the teams that react the quickest will have the opportunity to score as the opponent is transitioning into defence. Players will be engaged and ready to switch in on the coach's command.

COACHING NOTES
+ Coaching objectives – to have players play with positivity and creativity and demonstrate quick reactions to the ball.
+ Coaching tip – Consciously manage where the ball is played into to challenge certain players or one team or the other and challenge reactions.
+ Adaptations – Create different match ups by changing only one team.

+ 3v3 with goalkeepers.
+ Player immediately penetrates on the dribble.
+ The decision to dribble is a good one.

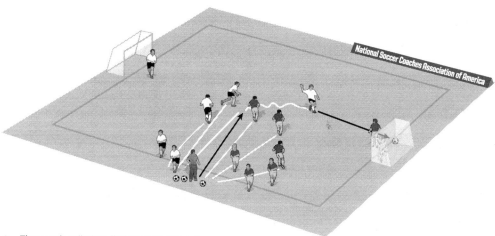

+ The coach calls for all players to sub out.
+ One player in white has responded quickest.
+ The urgency to get in is good and scores.

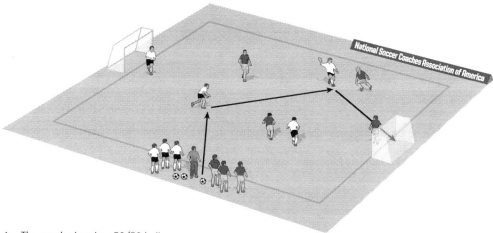

+ The coach plays in a 50/50 ball.
+ The white player immediately plays a penetrating forward pass.
+ The decision to pass quickly is a good one.

NUMBERS UP TO GOAL

STAGES COVERED BY ACTIVITY
Stages 3, 4 & 5 - 9-18 year old players

THEMES & COMPETENCIES
Theme:
+ Passing combinations
+ Attacking transition.
+ Defending in pairs and groups.
+ Shooting

Competencies:
+ Short passing along the ground (5-15 yards).
+ Receiving using the feet.
+ Mobility on and off the ball.
+ Attacking and defending as an individual.
+ Attacking and defending in pairs and small groups.
+ Attacking support.
+ Shooting technique

WHY USE IT
To encourage players to play direct to goal and to identify a 'numbers up' situation.

SET UP
30 x 25 yards with 1 goal. A goalkeeper and 2 teams of 4 players. Supply of balls and 2 sets of pinnies.

HOW TO PLAY
Play begins with 1 attacker v goalkeeper. Whatever the outcome, the attacking player becomes a defender. 2 attackers set off from the cones and attempt to score past the defender and goalkeeper. The defender steps off the field and re-joins the line. As before, once the ball is won by the defenders or a goal is scored, the 2 attackers now transition to being the defenders against the next 3 attacking players. The next progression is 4v3 and the final progression is 4v4. If the defenders win the ball they should return it to the coach as a counter option. Restart the game, switching out the goalkeeper.

COACHING NOTES
+ Coaching objectives – To encourage players to play incisively and quickly to goal.
+ Coaching tip – Encourage each new attack to begin immediately after the ball goes dead.
+ Adaptations – Add a points system – goal 2 points, defenders pass to coach or keeper saves 1 point.

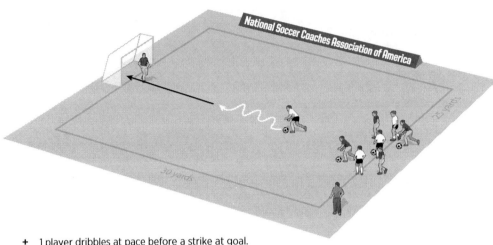

+ 1 player dribbles at pace before a strike at goal.
+ 2 opposing players are on deck to attack.

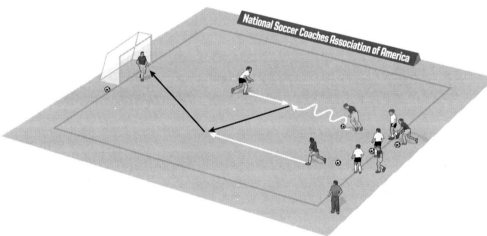

+ Attacker on the ball commits the defender.
+ 2nd attacker receives a pass for a shot at goal.

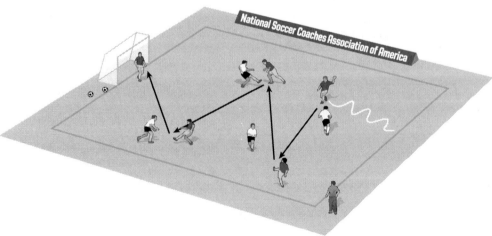

+ The game progresses to a 4v4.
+ The attacking team pass and move to create a shot

MIRROR GOAL

STAGES COVERED BY ACTIVITY
Stages 3, 4 & 5 - 9-18 year old players

THEMES & COMPETENCIES
Theme:
+ Shooting

Competencies:
+ Shooting technique

WHY USE IT
To encourage players to play direct to goal. The use of the Mirror Goal gives the players lots of opportunity to shoot at goal. It also allows for the efficient retrieval of balls and an opportunity for the coach to critically observe the players technique.

SET UP
Set up an appropriately sized goal using flags. 2 teams of 4 players, with a ball each are on either side of the goal. The distance from goal should be appropriate for the players technical level – start a distance of 20 yards and then modify.

HOW TO PLAY
One team provides a goalkeeper. The first player from the opposing team dribbles the ball forward and shoots before a cone marking a designated distance from goal. After the shot the shooter moves forward to be in goal and receives a shot from the other direction. The outgoing keeper is responsible for retrieving the ball and returns to their team. The first player in line from the other side now dribbles forward and shoots.

COACHING NOTES
+ Coaching objectives – to provide the players valuable repetition of striking a moving ball at goal.
+ Coaching tip – observe closely the position of the non-kicking foot and the head at the moment of impact as this will impact the strength and direction of the shot.
+ Adaptations – provide a server to challenge the players with both feet, different pace of the ball and different angles.

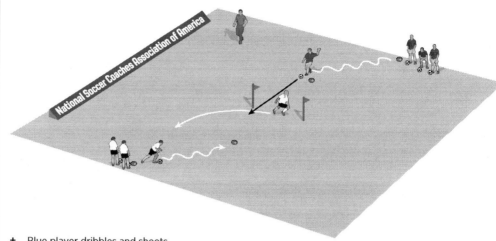

+ Blue player dribbles and shoots.
+ White goalkeeper recovers ball.
+ White shooter is ready to play.

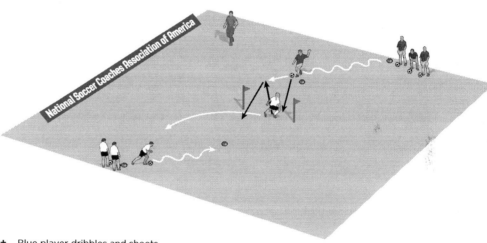

+ Blue player dribbles and shoots.
+ White goalkeeper gives up a rebound.
+ Blue player can finish rebound with one touch.

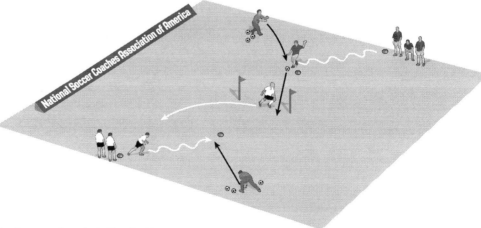

+ A server plays the ball to the blue player.
+ White goalkeeper retrieves the ball.
+ Immediately a server for white plays a ball forward.

2 VS 2 TO SMALL GOALS

STAGES COVERED BY ACTIVITY
Stages 3, 4 & 5 - 9-18 year old players

THEMES & COMPETENCIES
Theme:
+ Passing combinations
+ Attacking transition.
+ Defending in pairs and groups.
+ Shooting

Competencies:
+ Short passing along the ground (5-15 yards).
+ Receiving using the feet.
+ Mobility on and off the ball.
+ Attacking and defending as an individual.
+ Attacking and defending in pairs and small groups.
+ Attacking support.
+ Shooting technique

WHY USE IT
This activity gives pairs lots of repetition and opportunity to learn important principles of defending - pressure and cover.

SET UP
In a 20x12 yard grid place two small goals on a diagonal from each other. Play 2v2 inside the grid with the ball being introduced by a server each time.

HOW TO PLAY
Both pairs start in their own half of the field to begin. The server should favor one pair or the other with the ball. The other team must communicate who will pressure the ball and where they will direct the pressure – inside, outside or backwards. One player will pressure the ball and the other will provide cover to effectively double team.

COACHING NOTES
+ Coaching objectives – to train all players the fundamentals of small group defending. PRESSURE and COVER.
+ Coaching tip – vary the service and the start positions of players to create different scenarios for the players to defend.
+ Adaptations – replace goals with an end line to dribble in order to vary the challenge for the defending pair.

+ Closest blue player 'presses' white as the ball arrives.
+ 2nd blue player moves to cover teammate.

+ As white receives the first blue player 'presses'.
+ Blue pressure forces the attacker to the outside.
+ 2nd blue player runs to cover on the outside.

+ 2nd white player overlaps.
+ Blue pressure forces to inside.
+ 2nd blue player covers to inside.

SHOOTING CIRCLE

STAGES COVERED BY ACTIVITY
Stages 3, 4 & 5 - 9-18 year old players

THEMES & COMPETENCIES
Theme:
+ Passing combinations
+ Attacking transition.
+ Shooting

Competencies:
+ Short passing along the ground (5-15 yards).
+ Receiving using the feet.
+ Mobility on and off the ball.
+ Attacking as an individual.
+ Attacking in pairs.
+ Attacking support.
+ Shooting technique

WHY USE IT
This activity creates shooting frequency. The types of shooting scenarios can be varied and the coach can observe closely to provide individual instruction.

SET UP
Use 2 big goals with keepers. The distance between goals should provide an appropriate challenge. Start with groups of players at each goal with plenty of balls.

HOW TO PLAY
The ball is passed by the shooter to a target who lays it off for a shot. When the ball is dead the shooter becomes the target and the target retrieves the ball.

COACHING NOTES
+ Coaching objectives – to give the players repetitions for strikes at goal with a variety of service.
+ Coaching tip – encourage players to take a look at the goalkeeper's position as they move, without the ball, on to the shot. Head over the ball for the shot.
+ Adaptations – have the target spin and take the shot (diagram #3)

+ A pass made to a central target is laid off to the outside.
+ The shooter runs onto the ball.
+ The shooter attempts to score to the near or far post.

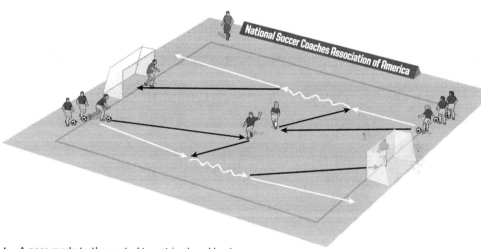

+ A pass made to the central target is played back.
+ Shooter must collect ball and dribble before shot.

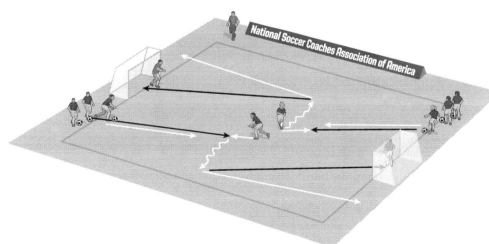

+ The target player checks to the ball, receives and turns.
+ The target player takes the shot on the turn then retrieves the ball.

DEFENDING THE CROSS

Stages 3, 4 & 5 - 9-18 year old players

THEMES & COMPETENCIES
Theme:
+ Defending in pairs and groups.
+ Shooting

Competencies:
+ Medium to long passing.
+ Receiving using the feet.
+ Mobility on and off the ball.
+ Attacking and defending as an individual.
+ Attacking and defending in pairs and small groups.
+ Shooting technique.

WHY USE IT
This activity helps train the goalkeeper and central defenders to organize for crosses served into the penalty area.

SET UP
The activity focuses on the penalty area. A server provides crosses to the forwards running from outside the area to goal - these crosses are unchallenged. Both the defenders and goalkeeper start goal side of the forwards. Flags are placed outside the area as a target for the defenders to aim the clearance towards.

HOW TO PLAY
Have the server signal a cross is to be served to begin the movement of the forwards. As the forwards move the defenders must respond to their movement, the flight of the ball and the direction of the goalkeeper.

COACHING NOTES
+ Coaching objectives – to train defenders to mark opponents on crosses and clear the ball.
+ Coaching tip – vary the starting points of the attackers and defenders to create different situations that will occur in the game.
+ Adaptations – increase the number of attackers and vary the position of the crosser.

+ Forwards move near and far post.
+ Defenders recover to deep and inside positions.

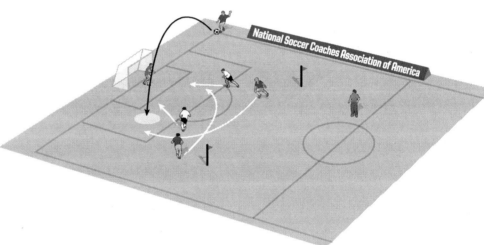

+ Forwards make crossing runs.
+ Defenders avoid crossing each other.
+ Defenders recover to goal.

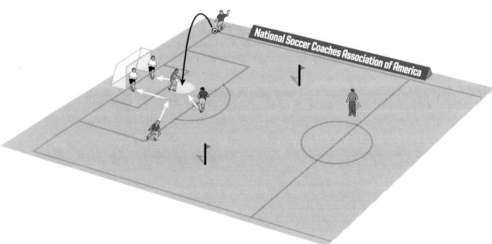

+ The goalkeeper calls for the ball and comes out.
+ Defenders recover to the goal line to cover the goalkeeper.

4 VS 2+2

STAGES COVERED BY ACTIVITY
Stages 3, 4 & 5 - 9-18 year old players

THEMES & COMPETENCIES
Theme:
+ Defending in pairs and groups.
+ Attacking transition.
+ Passing combinations.

Competencies:
+ Medium to long passing.
+ Receiving using the feet.
+ Mobility on and off the ball.
+ Attacking and defending as an individual.
+ Attacking and defending in pairs and small groups.

WHY USE IT
Activity works on pressure - cover and transition. It assists players in both communication and identifying situations that occur in the game.

SET UP
In a 15x15 yard grid start with 4 attackers with a ball and 2 defenders. 2 other defenders start outside the area.

HOW TO PLAY
Play a standard game of keep away – blues attempting to combine passes to keep the ball from the white defenders. The focus is on defending. Specifically, on the role of the first defender to press the ball and the second defender to provide cover – without giving up a 'splitting' pass between defenders. Include an incentive for the defenders that if they win the ball and can pass it out of the area to their team mates they can switch roles. Play can be continuous with coach supervision.

COACHING NOTES
+ Coaching objectives – to encourage the two defenders to work in tandem, to win possession and in transition play to their team mates in space.
+ Coaching tip – help the two defenders reminding them to make up space as the ball is traveling, rather than wait for the ball to arrive at an opponent.
+ Adaptations – as the defenders improve make the grid bigger to increase the challenge.

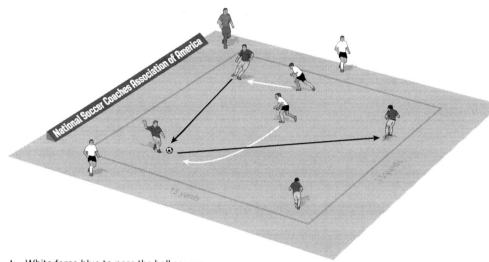

+ White force blue to pass the ball square.
+ Only one white player reacts.
+ Blue plays a splitting pass.

+ White players work together.
+ Blue is forced to pass square.
+ White players react together to apply pressure.

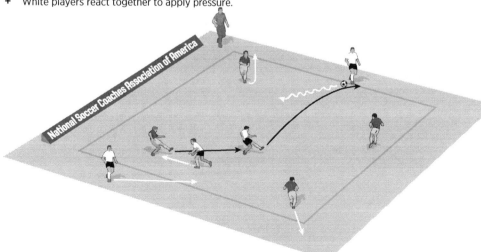

+ A white player intercepts the attempted splitting pass.
+ White players pass to their peripheral targets.
+ Teams switch roles.

RUN AND SHOOT

STAGES COVERED BY ACTIVITY
Stages 3, 4 & 5 - 9-18 year old players

THEMES & COMPETENCIES
Theme:
+ Defending in pairs and groups.
+ Attacking transition.
+ Passing combinations.
+ Shooting.

Competencies:
+ Medium to long passing.
+ Receiving using the feet.
+ Mobility on and off the ball.
+ Attacking and defending as an individual.
+ Attacking and defending in pairs and small groups.
+ Shooting technique

WHY USE IT
This activity allows for a lot of frequency of shooting under pressure. Attackers are rewarded for being direct. The target player adds combination options.

SET UP
2 big goals with keepers. Using 3 zones have a target for each team in the attacking zone. Have 4 players with 2 balls for each team in the middle zone.

HOW TO PLAY
Each team passes and moves with 2 balls. Players are numbered 1-4 for each team. When their color and number is called they attack the goal and the opposing number defends. Attackers can use the target for support. The target can finish rebounds.

COACHING NOTES
+ Coaching objectives – to increase confidence in front of goal under realistic pressure.
+ Coaching tip – encourage players to be positive in front of goal and not to pass up a clear chance.
+ Adaptations – call 2 numbers to attack and defend and/or have a defender on the target.

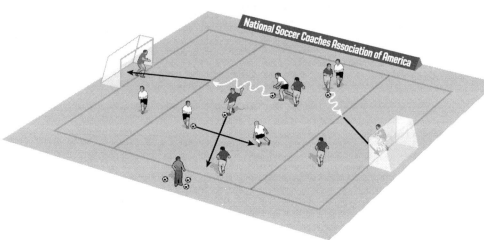

+ Defenders give immediate chase.
+ Attackers dribble and shoot under pressure.

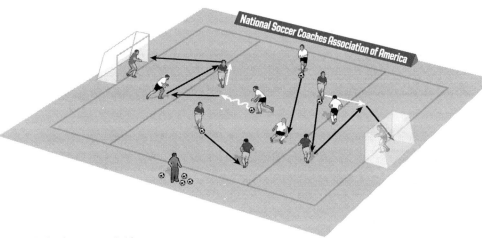

+ Defenders get goal side.
+ Attackers use targets to get shots off.

+ Shots on goal are saved by the goalkeepers.
+ Target players finish rebounds.

6 GOAL GAME

STAGES COVERED BY ACTIVITY
Stages 3, 4 & 5 - 9-18 year old players

THEMES & COMPETENCIES
Theme:
+ Defending in pairs and groups.
+ Attacking transition.
+ Passing combinations.

Competencies:
+ Medium to long passing.
+ Receiving using the feet.
+ Mobility on and off the ball.
+ Attacking and defending as an individual.
+ Attacking and defending in pairs and small groups.

WHY USE IT
This activity allows for realistic challenges to the defending team. To defend effectively players must demonstrate ability to pressure and cover.

SET UP
Have 3 cone goals for each team to defend. Behind those goals have a Goalkeeper who is a support player for the team in possession. Goalkeeper's begin each repetition.

HOW TO PLAY
The objective for the possession team, in conjunction with their supporting Goalkeeper, is to pass or dribble through one of the 3 cone goals. The opposing team must try to deny the score, win the ball and counter.

COACHING NOTES
+ Coaching objectives – to have effective defending at the point of the ball to allow for effective team defense.
+ Coaching tip – make sure your vision takes in all members of the defending team and can assess their positions.
+ Adaptations – employ an all-time attacking player to further challenge the defending team.

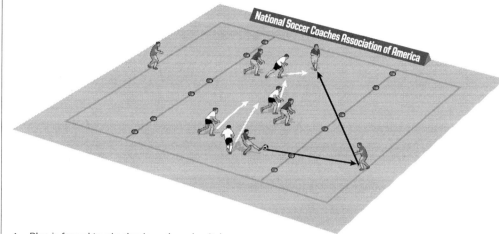

+ Blue is forced to play backwards and switch.
+ White reacts well to press and cover.

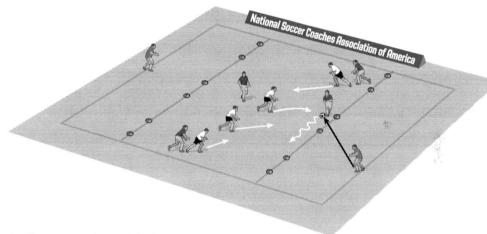

+ The entry pass is well defended.
+ Blue is forced to dribble into pressure.

+ Blue attacks on the dribble.
+ Pressure and cover forces a negative backward pass.

WIDE GATE GAME

STAGES COVERED BY ACTIVITY
Stages 3, 4 & 5 - 9-18 year old players

THEMES & COMPETENCIES
Theme:
+ Defending in pairs and groups.
+ Attacking transition.
+ Passing combinations.

Competencies:
+ Medium to long passing.
+ Receiving using the feet.
+ Mobility on and off the ball.
+ Attacking and defending as an individual.
+ Attacking and defending in pairs and small groups.

WHY USE IT
This activity encourages players to support passes they play forward. It reinforces the importance of width and mobility in the attack..

SET UP
Field is 30x25 with wide gates on the half way line. Two small goals with keepers and 3v3 on the field.

HOW TO PLAY
In each half there is a 2v1 advantage to the team defending that end. When the ball is played forward to the lone target, one of the deeper players must support by running forward through the gates.

COACHING NOTES
+ Coaching objectives – to have effective defending at the point of the ball to allow for effective team defense.
+ Coaching tip – make sure your vision takes in all members of the defending team and can assess their positions.
+ Adaptations – employ an all-time attacking player to further challenge the defending team.

+ White commits blue on the dribble.
+ The pass forward is followed by a wide run.

+ Blue penetrates on the dribble.
+ The blue target checks to the back post.

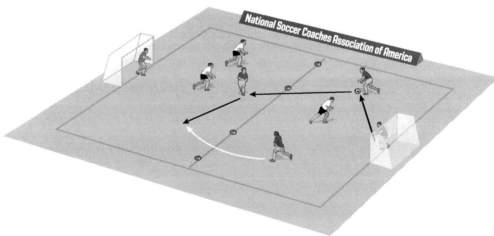

+ The ball is played forward to the target.
+ The third player moves off the ball to support.

HEX FIELD GAME

STAGES COVERED BY ACTIVITY
Stages 3, 4 & 5 - 9-18 year old players

THEMES & COMPETENCIES
Theme:
+ Defending in pairs and groups.
+ Attacking transition.
+ Passing combinations.
+ Shooting.

Competencies:
+ Medium to long passing.
+ Receiving using the feet.
+ Mobility on and off the ball.
+ Attacking and defending as an individual.
+ Attacking and defending in pairs and small groups.
+ Shooting technique.

WHY USE IT
This activity creates increased challenge the closer to goal players get. Players pick up their speed of play as they go forward.

SET UP
Field is 30x25 with each corner coned off to create a hexagon. Use two big goals with keepers and 3 v3 on the field.

HOW TO PLAY
Play is a regular scrimmage on the modified field. The zoned off corner space is out of bounds.

COACHING NOTES
+ Coaching objectives – to encourage players to increase their speed of play closer to goal as space diminishes.
+ Coaching tip – encourage width in the development phase of an attack to challenge the defending team.
+ Adaptations – use an all-time attacking player to improve success if need be, before getting to even numbers.

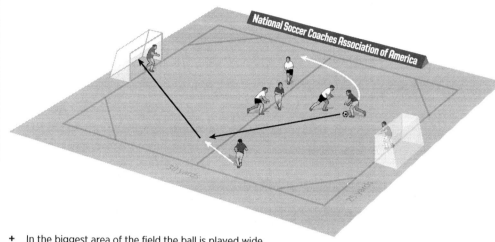

+ In the biggest area of the field the ball is played wide.
+ Attacking movement comes way from the ball.

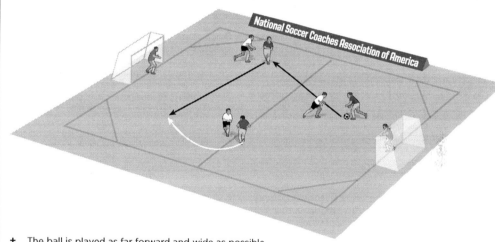

+ The ball is played as far forward and wide as possible.
+ Attacking runs are made centrally.

+ Play is developed from the back.
+ The attacking run is central.

PATTERN PLAY

STAGES COVERED BY ACTIVITY
Stages 3, 4 & 5 - 9-18 year old players

THEMES & COMPETENCIES
Theme:
+ Defending in pairs and groups.
+ Attacking transition.
+ Passing combinations.
+ Shooting.

Competencies:
+ Medium to long passing.
+ Receiving using the feet.
+ Mobility on and off the ball.
+ Attacking and defending as an individual.
+ Attacking and defending in pairs and small groups.
+ Shooting technique.

WHY USE IT
This activity helps the coach establish identifiable patterns of play for the team to put into practice. It can help teams develop a style.

SET UP
Field is 50x35. Use two big goals with plenty of balls, two keepers with five teammates each.

HOW TO PLAY
Starting with the keeper the team plays a sequence of unopposed passes toward their opponent's goal before shooting. They then reset and repeat. Both teams pass and move through each other.

COACHING NOTES
+ Coaching objectives – to develop patterns of passing and movement that translate into the game.
+ Coaching tip – encourage players to be technically clean and to always be moving forward in the possession.
+ Adaptations – go alternately at first if need be. Develop to having some opposition to each pattern.

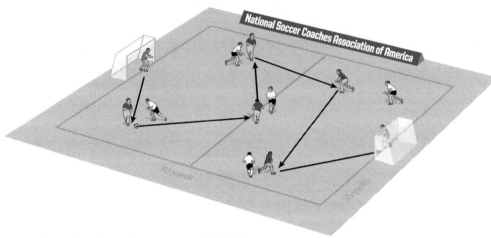

+ Ball begins wide and is played to a center mid.
+ Ball is switched twice before the shot.

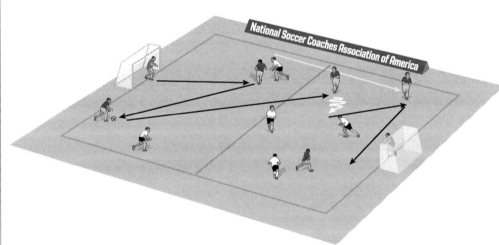

+ The ball begins centrally and is dropped back.
+ A long diagonal is supported by a deep overlap.

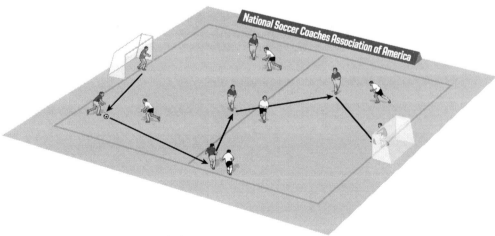

+ Play is developed down one flank.
+ The point of attack is switched from the center.

KNOCK AND MOVE

STAGES COVERED BY ACTIVITY

Stages 2, 3 & 4 - 6-14 year old players

THEMES & COMPETENCIES

Theme:
+ Passing combinations

Competencies:
+ Short passing along the ground (5-15 yards)
+ Receiving using the feet
+ Mobility on and off the ball.

WHY USE IT

To develop passing and passing receiving technique. To develop patterns of movement.

SET UP

Use four players 15-20 yards apart, with one player in positioned in the middle.

HOW TO PLAY

The activity is a 4 pass sequence, with 4 corresponding movements. Once the sequence is played it comes back the other way. The passing sequence involves four passes and four movements. The sequence goes back and forth and is continuous.

COACHING NOTES

+ Coaching objectives – to have players play the way they face and turn without the ball.
+ Coaching tip – make sure the spin movement of the middle player is wide, not long.
+ Adaptations – develop to a two or one touch sequence.

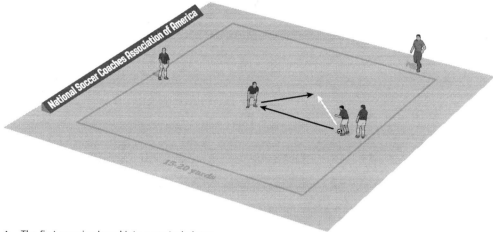

+ The first pass is played into a central player.
+ The passer moves off at an angle to receive the ball back.

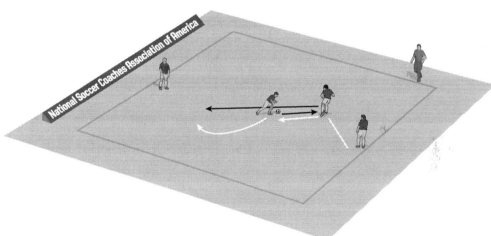

+ The central player makes a bending run wide and away.
+ The first passer plays the ball to the runner and moves to the central position.

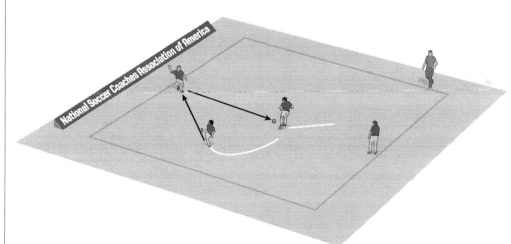

+ The ball is played to the player at the opposite end of the space.
+ The passer follows the pass.
+ The entire sequence of four passes and four movements then resets the other way.

STAGE 4: PLAYERS 12-14 YEARS OLD

Dramatic physical changes are the hallmark of adolescence. Late stage 3 and early stage 4, there will be noticeable differences occurring in the growth of girls in comparison to boys. Girls (12 years) generally experience peak growth approximately two years ahead of boys (14 years). Since many young adolescents are unaware that the onset and rate of puberty vary greatly, they need reassurance that their own growth and development is normal, and they will benefit from learning about the progression of physiological changes. Most 12-year-olds focus on social life, friends and school and they continue friendships with members of the same sex. Coaches must be sensitive to close friendships when selecting teams and generally working with children in stage 4 - emotional changes can enhance sensitivity and lead to conflicts between players and between players and adults.

DEVELOPMENT FOCUS

- On average, girls reach Peak Height Velocity (PHV) in Stage 4. Aerobic power should be introduced progressively after growth rate decelerates.
- Continue to consolidate the performance of fundamental and advanced individual skills.
- Players should receive more in-depth tactical instructions, particularly in understanding playing positions. Players should continue to experience different positions on the field.
- Optimum time for the introduction of Strength training for girls (immediately following PHV)
- A second speed training window opens for girls (11-13 years)
- The second speed training window opens for boys (13-16 years)
- Players should play other sports, but soccer should be the primary sport during the soccer season for the serious and committed.

KEY DEVELOPMENT POINTS FOR CHILDREN IN STAGE 4		
Physically	**Psychological/Social**	**Cognitive/Mental**
1. Boys – Stage 4 is the most likely time when boys start going through puberty.	1. Emotional development may not correlate to physical development – physical changes may occur earlier and develop more rapidly.	1. Players are able to think abstractly, and are able to contribute to critical thinking
2. Girls – late developers start puberty at this stage but for many girls the later stage is the conclusion of puberty.	2. Continued development of independence, yet wants and needs adult help.	2. Player can become more egotistical – resulting in increased awareness of personal performance successes and failures.
3. Significant proportional changes occur in bone, muscle and fat.	3. Players may start to question coaches and parents more readily and become less accepting - Less affection may be shown toward adults and players may sometimes seem rude or short tempered.	3. A heightened sense of personal achievement and striving for perfection/ success.
4. Extremities grow quicker than the trunk resulting in a gangling appearance.		4. Players have more capabilities for complex thought.
5. Decreases in flexibility occur.		5. Better able to express feelings through talking.
6. Oxygen transportation is greatly improved due to increased production of red blood cells – aiding aerobic energy production.	4. Hormones become more active and can lead to mood swings and behavioral fluctuations.	6. A stronger sense of right and wrong.
7. The nervous system is almost fully developed.	5. Players are more interested in and influenced by peer group - Increasingly concerned about acceptance by friends.	7. Ready for in-depth, longer learning experiences.
8. Displays rapid but uneven physical growth, leading at times to awkwardness, uncoordinated movement, tiredness, lack of confidence and poor posture.	6. Peer group becomes increasingly important in fostering independence and interaction with members of the opposite sex.	8. Has a continuing need for reinforcement and development of self-esteem, especially in relation to body perception and sport.
9. Increase in female and male hormone levels	7. Players become more concerned about body image, looks and clothes.	9. Increasingly capable of making informed decisions and accepting a leadership role, although often may choose not to do so.
10. Increase in height, weight and musculature.	8. Focus on self, going back and forth between high expectations and lack of confidence.	10. Requires opportunities to be creative and may need consistent encouragement.
11. Males develop deeper voices, characteristic patterns of facial/body hair become stronger.	9. Eating problems sometimes start at this stage – resulting in reduced energy and poor performance.	11. Can concentrate and participate in activities for longer periods of time.
12. Females become wider at hips; breast development continues for several years.	10. Shows tolerance of needs and abilities of others.	
13. Girls may reach close to physical maturity.		

DEVELOPMENT CHARACTERISTICS TRANSLATED TO COACHING PLAYERS IN STAGE 4

Developing a team of players with large individual performance differences can create significant headaches for coaches. Pressure to prepare a team to compete against teams from different towns can often overshadow the needs of individual players. There is still a considerable amount for the players to learn as they are exposed to advanced techniques and team tactics. Players entering Stage 4 with competency in the basic skills are well placed to develop quickly. The hours spent developing individual mastery of the ball will pay dividends as the coach introduces activities where solid techniques are prerequisites for success.

TRANSLATED TO PLAYER DEVELOPMENT THIS MEANS

1. Provide players with a variety of experiences by coaching them how to play a number of positions.

2. Educate players on the physical, cognitive and emotional changes occurring.

3. Dynamic stretches prior to activity and static stretches following – flexibility naturally deteriorates so efforts must be made to regain range of motion.

4. Players should be given opportunity to play and train with others of similar ability.

5. Conditions for aerobic training are right – increasing aerobic capacity will allow players to perform high intensity (anaerobic) activities more frequently and recovery will be quicker.

6. As the nervous system becomes refined, performing correct technique is essential.

7. Continue to focus on individual ball mastery.

8. Tactical focus must be determined based on readiness of the individuals.

9. Players should be exposed to different positions and different roles.

10. Psychological training can be introduced such as coping strategies and mental imagery.

11. Bear in mind that early and late development has different implications for males and females.

12. Sessions should reinforce communication as an essential team skill.

13. Involve players in decision making and analysis of individual and team performance.

14. Create opportunities for team building.

15. Work with the players on attack and defensive strategies.

16. Speak to parents to ensure they understand and support the training methods employed.

17. Players should be working on flexibility, speed, endurance and strength – strength activities should be using their own body weight, Swiss Balls and Medicine Balls.

18. The first training window for speed and strength for female players occurs immediately after peak height velocity.

19. The only training window for speed and strength for male players opens 12-18 months after peak height velocity.

3V1 KEEP-AWAY IN A GRID

STAGES COVERED BY ACTIVITY
Stages 3, 4 & 5 - 9-18 year old players

THEMES & COMPETENCIES
Theme:
+ Transition and attacking rhythm
+ Switching the point of attack

Competencies:
+ Short passing along the ground
+ Receiving using the feet
+ Mobility on and off the ball.
+ Attacking in pairs and small groups.
+ Defending as an individual.

WHY USE IT
This exercise works on maintaining ball possession in tight spaces, emphasizes proper body shape to protect the ball when passing and receiving, and challenges players to quickly provide close support to their teammates.

SET UP
Set up four cones to mark a 10x10 yard box. Position 3 players on the perimeter of the grid with one ball.

HOW TO PLAY
Begin by playing 3v0 in a Grid. Players are limited to 2 or 3 touches on the ball. They pass the ball to each other around the perimeter as quickly as they can. As each pass is made, the other player must sprint to fix the supporting shape (so that options always exist to the right and left of the dribbler). Progress the activity by adding a central defender who holds a vest. If the defender intercepts the ball, or an attacker commits a "thinking foul" (takes too many touches or uses the incorrect passing surface), then the defender throws the vest at the feet of the offending player and trades roles.

COACHING NOTES
+ Coaching objectives - Require players to use only the inside of the outside foot to make each pass and look for players to open their hips to see the entire grid as they receive the ball
+ Coaching tip - Call "thinking fouls" for the players originally, then shift the responsibility to the defender to look for these mistakes
+ Adaptations - Everyone must work to keep the ball alive. If it stops rolling for any reason, all 4 players must do two quick push-ups.

+ Player with the ball has support right and left.
+ Players must sprint to fix the supporting shape.

+ Add a defender.
+ Defender trades roles with an attacker on interceptions or "thinking fouls"

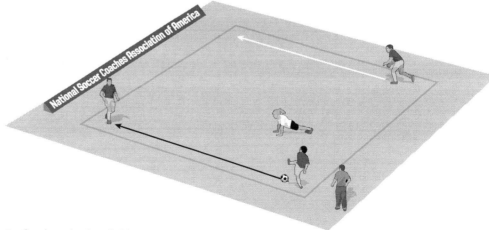

+ Coach randomly calls "time!"
+ Have the defender do 5 sit-ups/push-ups before trading roles.

TARGET BOXES SCRIMMAGE

STAGES COVERED BY ACTIVITY
Stages 3, 4 & 5 - 9-18 year old players

THEMES & COMPETENCIES
Theme:
+ Transition and attacking rhythm
+ Switching the point of attack

Competencies:
+ Short and medium passing
+ Receiving using different surfaces of the body.
+ Mobility on and off the ball.
+ Attacking in pairs and small groups.
+ Defending in pairs and small groups.

WHY USE IT
This activity focuses on improving awareness and vision of the field, and helps encourage players to switch the point of attack.

SET UP
Using cones, set up 4 small (2x2 yard) "target boxes" in a larger 20x20 yard playing area. Designate two opposing grids as the "white" boxes, and the other two grids as the "blue" boxes. Form two teams to play 5v5. Place a player in each target box, and play 3v3 in the area around the boxes.

HOW TO PLAY
Teams score goals by completing a pass to either of the two teammates in their target boxes. The target player must control the pass cleanly (entirely within the box), and no defenders can enter the box. When a point is scored, the receiving player dribbles out of the target box and is replaced by the teammate who made the previous pass into the box. The attackers now try to score by passing to the target player in the opposite box.

COACHING NOTES
+ Coaching objectives - Focus on awareness of open space and numbers-up v numbers down areas. Look for the long option first, but use closer options to keep possession if a penetrating pass is not open. The best pass may be behind you!
+ Coaching tip - Demand technical precision for passes and first touches!
+ Adaptation - Increase numbers and space to play 4v4 in the middle.

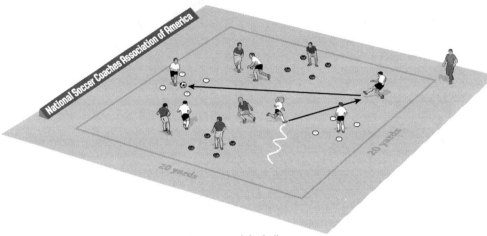

+ Use the dribble to create 2v1 situations around the ball.
+ Score first if possible; keep possession otherwise.

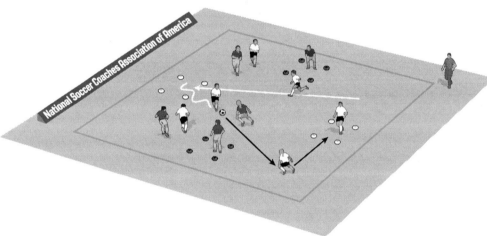

+ Transition roles quickly after each scoring pass.
+ The team must now attack the opposite target box.

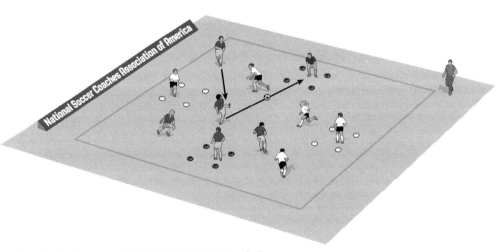

+ Attack either target box when you first win the ball.
+ Keep score and put an incentive on the line to win!

STAGES COVERED BY ACTIVITY

Stages 3, 4 & 5 - 9-18 year old players

THEMES & COMPETENCIES

Theme:
+ Transition and attacking rhythm
+ Switching the point of attack

Competencies:
+ Short and medium passing
+ Receiving using different surfaces of the body.
+ Mobility on and off the ball.
+ Attacking in pairs and small groups.
+ Defending in pairs and small groups.

WHY USE IT

This game helps train players to read an opponent's defensive shape, and encourages them to change the point of attack in midfield to find better attacking options.

SET UP

Set up a 30 yard (long) x 60 yard (wide) field with 3 sets of cone goals placed along each end. The 2 cone goals in the center of the field should be only 2-3 yards wide; the other 4 goals (near each corner of the field) should be 6-8 yards wide.

HOW TO PLAY

Play a game of 6v6, with each team defending 3 goals and attacking the other 3 goals.

COACHING NOTES

+ Coaching objectives – Look for players to have "their heads on swivels" to be aware of options to the right and left. Play the way you are facing whenever possible.
+ Coaching tip – Note that the shape of this game naturally reinforces the topic, as it requires players to use more width than length to be successful.
+ Adaptations – Play without the 2 central cone gates.

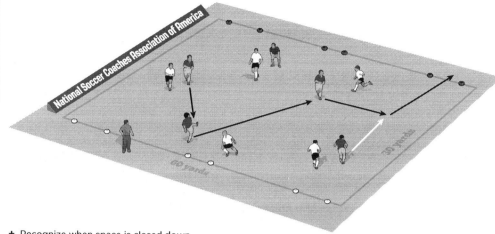

+ Recognize when space is closed down.
+ Work the ball quickly toward open space.

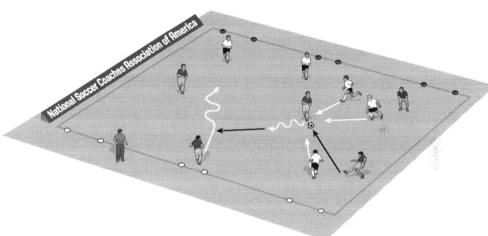

+ Look around before the ball arrives.
+ Turn away from pressure in the middle of the field with the first touch.

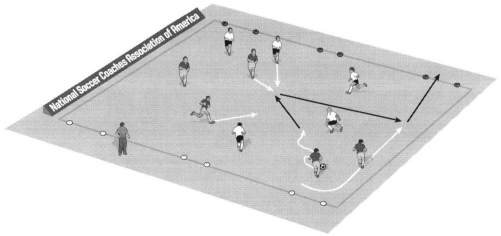

+ When numbers-up, attack the goal and score!

FOUR GOAL GAME WITH GOALKEEPERS

STAGES COVERED BY ACTIVITY

Stages 3, 4 & 5 - 9-18 year old players

THEMES & COMPETENCIES

Theme:
+ Transition and attacking rhythm
+ Switching the point of attack
+ Counter attacking and finishing breakaways

Competencies:
+ Short and medium passing
+ Receiving using different surfaces of the body.
+ Mobility on and off the ball.
+ Attacking in pairs and small groups.
+ Defending in pairs and small groups.
+ Shooting technique

WHY USE IT

This game creates many different opportunities for players to switch the point of attack and finish on a large goal, while incorporating goalkeepers into your team training.

SET UP

Using a 60x60 yard area, place a large goal in the center of each boundary line. Place a goalkeeper in each goal, and divide your field players into 2 teams.

HOW TO PLAY

Play 8v8 (including 2 keepers for each team), with each team defending 2 adjacent goals and attempting to score on the other 2.

COACHING NOTES

+ Coaching objectives – Take advantage of scoring opportunities whenever possible, and switch the point of attack when faced with an organized, compact defense. Emphasize good, frequent communication ("turn!", "man on!", "back!", "switch!", "again!").
+ Coaching tip – Keep extra balls near each goal so you can restart play quickly when shots go out of play.
+ Adaptations – If numbers aren't perfect, use a "full-time offense" player, or add "bumper" players to the corners of the playing area.

+ With numbers-down around the ball, switch the point of attack.

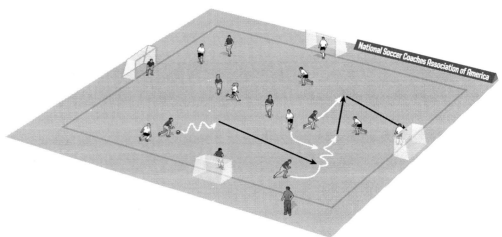

+ When numbers-up, go to goal and finish!

+ Goalkeepers must support the attack, too!
+ Goalkeepers first touch with the feet is away from pressure, then pass to a teammate.

HALF FIELD BARRIER SCRIMMAGE

STAGES COVERED BY ACTIVITY
Stages 3, 4 & 5 - 9-18 year old players

THEMES & COMPETENCIES
Theme:
+ Transition and attacking rhythm
+ Switching the point of attack
+ Counter attacking and finishing breakaways

Competencies:
+ Short and medium passing
+ Receiving using different surfaces of the body.
+ Mobility on and off the ball.
+ Attacking in pairs and small groups.
+ Defending in pairs and small groups.
+ Shooting technique

WHY USE IT
This match-related game requires teams to attack down the wings, and also challenges players to recognize the right moments to change the point of attack.

SET UP
A goal on the halfway line and another goal opposite on the goal line. Cone off a 40-yard-wide barrier midway between the goals. Divide players into 2 teams and play 8v8 in the half field - a goalkeeper in each goal. One goalkeeper has a ball.

HOW TO PLAY
Goalkeeper starts. Players can travel through the barrier but the ball must go around it. Goalkeepers can distribute the ball only by throwing it. If the ball crosses over or through the barrier, then play is restarted at the spot where the ball was last touched by a player on the opposing team. Play within the marked touchline and goal line boundaries, and enforce the offside law in each team's attacking half.

COACHING NOTES
+ Coaching objectives – Look for players to play through 4 tactical lines (GK/D/MF/F) while also using the full width of the field to maximize the available attacking space.
+ Coaching tip – Require 2 forwards to stay in the attacking half so that teams can't "pack the box" defensively and have distribution outlets when they win the ball
+ Adaptations – You can open a small hole in the center of the barrier to give a third attacking option down the middle of the field.

+ The keeper initiates action with a throw.
+ Attackers look to get the ball wide, then forward.

+ When one wing is closed down, switch the point of attack quickly through the backs.

+ Get deep to the goal line to set up drop-back passes
+ A trailing teammate should finish from a good shooting angle and distance

SPEED DRIBBLING ON A LINE

STAGES COVERED BY ACTIVITY

Stages 2, 3, & 4 - 6-14 year old players

THEMES & COMPETENCIES

Theme:
+ Transition and attacking rhythm
+ Counter attacking and finishing breakaways

Competencies:
+ Individual attacking
+ Running with the ball

WHY USE IT

This activity helps teach the proper technique for dribbling into open spaces at maximum speed while retaining control of the ball.

SET UP

Players line up at the end of any long line marked on the field (such as the top of the penalty area, or the halfway line). Each player should have a ball.

HOW TO PLAY

On the coach's command, the players dribble as fast as possible straight ahead, using the line on the field as a guide.

COACHING NOTES

+ Coaching objectives – The objective is to maximize their dribbling pace, so players should take several steps between each touch on the ball. They should also strike the ball firmly with either the laces or the outside of the same foot each time to keep the ball moving in stride.
+ Coaching tip – Use the existing field markings to see how straight each player can dribble on a sprint.
+ Adaptation – Add a small cone gate 20-25 yards away from the starting point, and challenge players to dribble through the gate using exactly three touches.

+ Use a "big" first touch to cover 6-8 yards before taking a second touch on the ball
+ The next player begins once the previous dribbler is 6-8 yards ahead

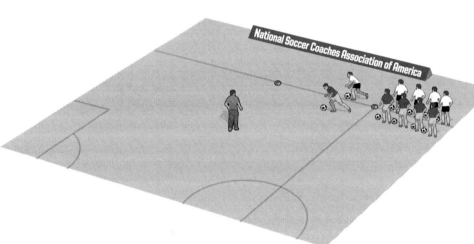

+ Players can race side-by-side to add competition to the activity

+ Add a gate to represent a target zone for the dribbler to attack
+ Give each player six attempts to reach the gate in exactly three touches
+ Keep score!

1V1 BREAKAWAYS TO GOAL

STAGES COVERED BY ACTIVITY

Stages 3, 4 & 5 - 9-18 year old players

THEMES & COMPETENCIES

Theme:
+ Transition and attacking rhythm
+ Counter attacking and finishing breakaways

Competencies:
+ Individual attacking
+ Running with the ball
+ Shooting technique

WHY USE IT

This activity allows players to practice finishing breakaways to goal with trailing pressure.

SET UP

Set up two cones near midfield, both at an angle to the goal, with one cone approximately 3 yards behind the other. The players lined up behind the cone closest to goal are the attackers, and should each have a ball. Use flags or poles to mark corner target zones 2 yards inside each post.

HOW TO PLAY

The first attacker starts the breakaway by dribbling to goal, and the first player on the other cone chases the attacker and attempts to cut him off before he can shoot. Switch lines so all players get several opportunities to be an attacker and defender. The player scoring the most goals (in the corners only) before time expires wins.

COACHING NOTES

+ Coaching objectives – Attack the goal at speed, get "between the pipes" as quickly as possible, and never stop your own breakaway by cutting the ball back.
+ Coaching tip – Don't use a goalkeeper so you can have multiple groups going at once from different angles.
+ Adaptations – Change the starting positions for both attackers and defenders so that the breakaways start from different angles, and so that pressure comes from different angles.

+ Play begins when the attacker takes the first touch on the ball.
+ Encourage the attackers to fake the first touch at times to keep the defenders "honest".

+ The attack ends if the defender succeeds in stopping the dribbler's forward momentum.
+ Shots must be scored in the corners; anything down the middle is considered "saved".

+ Change the starting positions of attackers and defenders to mimic different game scenarios
+ Keep score, and recognize the winners.

4V2 BREAKAWAYS TO GOAL

STAGES COVERED BY ACTIVITY

Stages 3, 4 & 5 - 9-18 year old players

THEMES & COMPETENCIES

Theme:
+ Transition and attacking rhythm
+ Switching the point of attack
+ Counter attacking and finishing breakaways

Competencies:
+ Short and medium passing
+ Receiving using different surfaces of the body.
+ Mobility on and off the ball.
+ Attacking in pairs and small groups.
+ Defending in pairs and small groups.
+ Shooting technique

WHY USE IT

This exercise focuses on improving your players skill at creating and supporting breakaways with "numbers up" in the attacking third of the field.

SET UP

Position a server (with balls) approximately 45 yards out from the goal, and put a keeper in goal. Use cones to mark a restraining line 30 yards out from the goal. Set up four attackers and two defenders in the midfield zone, in front of the cones, facing the server.

HOW TO PLAY

The server begins by passing a ball to one of the four attackers. The attackers use crossover runs, overlapping runs, and wall passes to create a breakaway that results in a quick shot on goal. The defenders can score by winning the ball and completing a pass back to the server, but they cannot drop past the cone line until the ball has entered the final zone.

COACHING NOTES

+ Coaching objectives – The attackers need to use quick ball movement and find penetrating passes to create breakaways for their teammates.
+ Coaching tip – Use another coach or player as an assistant referee to help enforce the offside law!
+ Adaptations – First increase the difficulty for the attackers by adding a third defender, then remove the high restraining line.

+ An attacker checks back to receive an entry pass from the server
+ All 4 attackers must be mobile to open seams for penetrating passes or dribbles

+ To create from the flanks, first move the ball to a wide position.
+ Use an early forward cross to initiate a breakaway down the middle.

+ To create from the center, first isolate a single defender with a dribble.
+ Use combination play and overlapping runs to spring a teammate through the defense.

SIT-UP SOCCER

STAGES COVERED BY ACTIVITY

Stages 3, 4 & 5 - 9-18 year old players

THEMES & COMPETENCIES
Theme:
+ Transition and attacking rhythm
+ Switching the point of attack
+ Counter attacking and finishing breakaways

Competencies:
+ Short and medium passing
+ Receiving using different surfaces of the body.
+ Mobility on and off the ball.
+ Attacking in pairs and small groups.
+ Defending in pairs and small groups.
+ Shooting technique

WHY USE IT
This is a fun, competitive game for your players to play while requiring them to focus on the quick transition between offense and defense.

SET UP
Set up two goals across half a field. Divide players into two teams, with one team wearing vests.

HOW TO PLAY
Play a normal game of 6v6 or 7v7 (including keepers). If any player on the team without the ball merely touches the ball, or if the attacking team loses possession in any way, then everyone on the attacking team must drop down and do one sit-up while the other team gets control of the ball and quickly counter-attacks. The players doing sit-ups must get up quickly to recover defensively.

COACHING NOTES
+ Coaching objectives – Focus on playing the ball forward quickly, immediately after winning possession during the brief moment when the opposing players are on the ground.
+ Coaching tip – The breakaway won't always be "on", so help players recognize when to counter quickly and when to possess the ball.
+ Adaptations – Expand the game to play full field, 11v11.

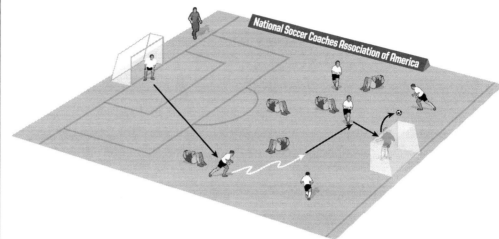

+ When the keeper makes a save, this is a loss of possession by the opponent.
+ The attackers now look to counter while the defenders perform a sit-up.

+ Focus on maintaining possession when the defenders are organized.
+ If a penetrating option opens up use it!

+ There are no sit-ups after scoring a goal!

8V8 RAPID ATTACK TO FULL GOALS

STAGES COVERED BY ACTIVITY

Stages 3, 4 & 5 - 9-18 year old players

THEMES & COMPETENCIES

Theme:
+ Transition and attacking rhythm
+ Switching the point of attack
+ Counter attacking and finishing breakaways

Competencies:
+ Short and medium passing
+ Receiving using different surfaces of the body.
+ Mobility on and off the ball.
+ Attacking in pairs and small groups.
+ Defending in pairs and small groups.
+ Shooting technique

WHY USE IT

This game trains your team to push out of the back quickly on transition from defense to offense.

SET UP

On a full-length field, place a goal on the top of each penalty area to create a 2/3-length field. Divide your players into two teams, with one wearing vests.

HOW TO PLAY

Play a game of 8v8 (7v7 plus goalkeepers). Require each team to have all 7 field players in the attacking half of the field before they can shoot on goal to score.

COACHING NOTES

+ Coaching objectives – This restriction will force your players to move forward quickly on transition to support the attack.
+ Coaching tip – By forcing all defenders to start from a high position up the field, this game naturally creates space behind the defense in which to counter-attack.
+ Adaptations – Expand to 11v11 and play with the same restriction on a full-length field.

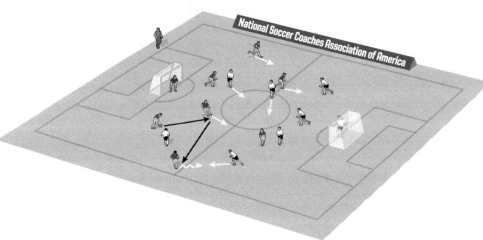

+ After regaining possession, there should be space to attack behind the opposing defenders.
+ All field players must rush forward into the attacking half before scoring.

+ Match direct passes with diagonal runs.
+ Direct passes generally don't work with direct runs!

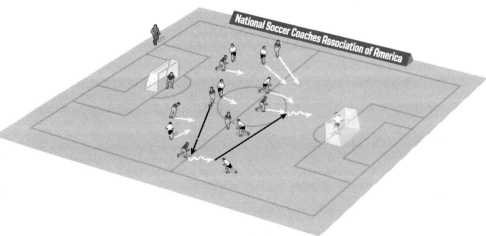

+ Match diagonal passes with direct or opposing diagonal runs.
+ Early forward crosses from deep positions can create dangerous breakaways!

5V2 KEEP AWAY

STAGES COVERED BY ACTIVITY
Stages 3, 4 & 5 - 9-18 year old players

THEMES & COMPETENCIES
Theme:
+ Transition and attacking rhythm
+ Switching the point of attack
+ Counter attacking and finishing breakaways
+ Group defending.

Competencies:
+ Short and medium passing
+ Receiving using different surfaces of the body.
+ Mobility on and off the ball.
+ Attacking in pairs and small groups.
+ Defending in pairs and small groups.
+ Shooting technique

WHY USE IT
This activity emphasizes defending in pairs, focusing on pressure and cover.

SET UP
5 attacking players in a circle with 2 defenders in the center holding a vest.

HOW TO PLAY
Play 5v2 keep-away, with a "minimum 2-touch" restriction for the outside possession players. If a player makes a poor pass, loses the ball to a defender, or violates the touch restriction, that player switches with one of the defenders and play continues immediately. If the attackers can "split" the defenders with a pass, the defenders must do 2 push-ups right away.

COACHING NOTES
+ Coaching objectives – Defenders to work as a unit to limit passing and penetrating options - using good pressure, cover, and communication. Defenders will usually be most successful if they trade between pressure and cover roles, and not "chase the ball".
+ Coaching tip – To increase competitiveness, randomly call "time" and have the two players in the middle do push-ups before trading out and restarting action.
+ Adaptations – Periodically adjust the touch restrictions, and include a requirement that the "ball must never die".

+ The first pass is "free", then the defenders attempt to win the ball
+ The defenders alternate pressure and cover roles

+ With a minimum touch restriction, attacking players are free to dribble
+ When the coach calls "time", the two players in the middle lose that round

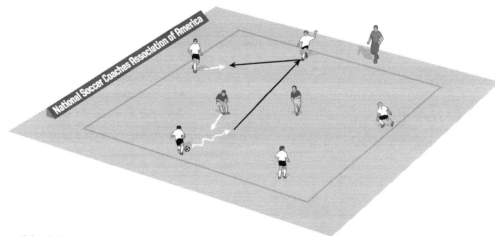

+ If the defenders are split by a pass, they must do 2 push-ups immediately
+ Play continues while the defenders are on the ground doing their push-ups

HUMAN FOOSBALL

STAGES COVERED BY ACTIVITY
Stages 4 & 5 - 12-18 year old players

THEMES & COMPETENCIES
Theme:
+ Group defending.

Competencies:
+ Defending in pairs and small groups.

WHY USE IT
This activity allows you to introduce and reinforce zonal defending principles.

SET UP
Use cones to mark four adjacent rectangular zones, each measuring 5x25 yards. Use vests to divide your players into a blue team and a white team. Place 4 players from the blue team in Zones 1 & 3, and 4 players from the white team in Zones 2 & 4. Have a supply of balls ready nearby.

HOW TO PLAY
Players must stay in their assigned zones and must not trade places laterally among their teammates. Play keep-away with one ball, where each team tries to score points by completing passes across their opponent's middle zone. Impose a "maximum 3-touch" restriction. The first team to reach 21 points wins. Swap players between the inside and outside zones and play again.

COACHING NOTES
+ Coaching objectives – Focus on communication among the defenders to organize pressure and cover. Look for proper body shape, angles of approach, and compact units to limit penetrating passing options.
+ Coaching tip – Players may pass within their own zone to change the point of attack and probe for penetrating passing lanes.
+ Adaptations – Remove the touch restriction and allow players to interchange positions within their zones.

+ Attacking players can move the ball within their zone
+ Attackers try to complete passes across the defenders zone to score points

+ The defenders must shift as a group to close down penetrating options
+ Quick communication is vital to ensure players recognize their proper roles

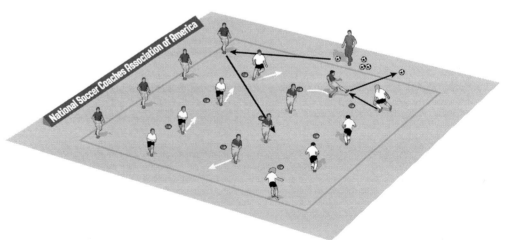

+ If a ball is knocked out of play, the coach serves a new ball in right away

3V3 IMMEDIATE CHASE TO GOAL

STAGES COVERED BY ACTIVITY
Stages 3, 4 & 5 - 9-18 year old players

THEMES & COMPETENCIES
Theme:
+ Group defending.
+ Counter attacking and finishing breakaways

Competencies:
+ Defending in pairs and small groups.
+ Mobility on and off the ball.
+ Attacking in pairs and small groups.
+ Shooting technique

WHY USE IT
This exercise improves your players ability to recover defensively when caught numbers-down in transition.

SET UP
Using cones, mark a grid measuring 30x30 yards, centered in the penalty area. Place a cone 10 yards outside the area. Start with 2 attackers, a goalkeeper, and a defender in the grid. Another attacker and 2 defenders start by the cone outside the grid. The single attacker has a ball.

HOW TO PLAY
The first attacker initiates action with a pass to one of his 2 teammates. The defenders are free to react as soon as the ball is in play. The 3 attackers work to score and the defenders work to win possession and counter attack. Enforce the offside law inside the grid.

COACHING NOTES
+ Coaching objectives – Look for the initial defender to delay and deny penetration as the other defenders work hard to recover into good positions quickly.
+ Coaching tip – Have an assistant coach watch the offside line closely so the defenders can employ a higher restraining line.
+ Adaptations – Begin with 2 defenders in the grid and just 1 recovering defender.

+ Play begins with an entry pass to an attacker in the grid
+ The first defender delays penetration as the other defenders recover

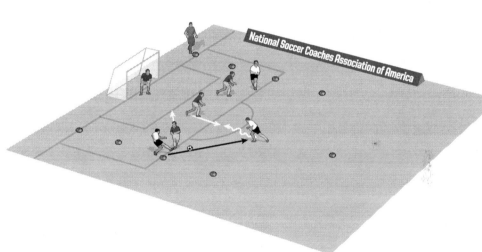

+ The recovering defenders must get goal-side and ball-side as quickly as possible
+ Once they have recovered, the defenders can step to the ball more aggressively

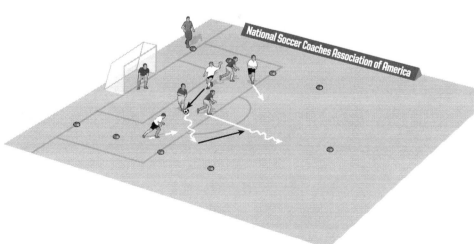

+ When the defenders win the ball, they work the ball out of the back

5V5+GK HALF FIELD GAME

THEMES & COMPETENCIES
Theme:
+ Group defending.
+ Counter attacking and finishing breakaways

Competencies:
+ Defending in pairs and small groups.
+ Mobility on and off the ball.
+ Attacking in pairs and small groups.
+ Shooting technique

WHY USE IT
This activity focuses on the coordination of defensive play across 2 tactical lines.

SET UP
Use cones to narrow half a full-sized field to the width of the penalty area. The attacking team of 5 players and defensive team of 5 field players plus a goalkeeper take the field. Both teams line up in a 3-2 formation. Position two wide target players near the halfway line, each with a supply of balls. Place an assistant coach on the touchline to enforce the offside law.

HOW TO PLAY
Play begins when one of the target players passes a ball to a midfielder on the attacking team. The attackers work to score. The defensive team works to win possession of the ball and then deliver a pass to either target player. Award 3 points for any goal scored by the attackers and 1 point for each pass made accurately to the target players by the defenders.

COACHING NOTES
+ Coaching objectives – Coach defensive play on both sides of the ball, with the 2 advance players giving initial pressure and limiting options as the back 3 players provide cover and balance.
+ Coaching tip – The use of midfield target players trains defenders to transition to attack quickly once they win the ball.
+ Adaptations – Increase the numbers to 6v5+GK.

+ Once the ball is in play, the first defender applies pressure and limits penetrating options

+ When a forward checks back to the ball, the defenders must coordinate their response

+ When the defenders win the ball, they transition to the attack immediately
+ The defenders score by completing a pass to either target player

3 TEAM KEEP-AWAY

STAGES COVERED BY ACTIVITY
Stages 3, 4 & 5 - 9-18 year old players

THEMES & COMPETENCIES
Theme:
+ Group defending.
+ Transition and attacking rhythm

Competencies:
+ Short and medium distance passing.
+ Receiving using different surfaces of the body.
+ Mobility on and off the ball.
+ Attacking in pairs and small groups.
+ Defending in pairs and small groups.

WHY USE IT
This game challenges players to be alert on transitions and imposes a significant cognitive demand on all active players.

SET UP
Split your players into three teams of 4 players per team, with each team wearing a different color vest.

HOW TO PLAY
In 1/4 field, one team plays defense and the other two teams combine as one team to play keep-away. Players have a "maximum 3-touch" restriction. If the defending team wins the ball, they join with the team that didn't lose the ball and the team that lost the ball immediately becomes the new defending team. The coach randomly calls "time", the team on defense at that moment loses the round.

COACHING NOTES
+ Coaching objectives – players recognizing moments of transition and work to offer short and long support to the player with the ball.
+ Coaching tip – Initially, help the players recognize transition moments by calling the color of the team that has just lost the ball and must now defend. Later, require all the players to call the color out instead of the coach doing it.
+ Adaptations – Require your players to make each pass to a player on the other offensive team. For example, if White and Blue have the ball and Green is defending, each White player must pass to someone on Blue (and vice versa).

+ Two teams of 4 players combine to play 8v4 keep-away in a grid

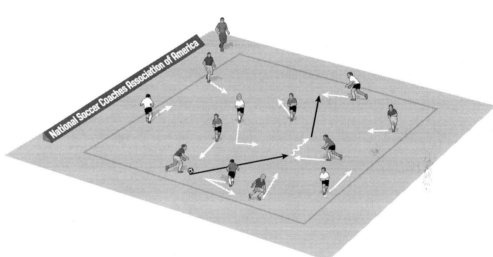

+ When the defenders win the ball, they immediately trade roles with the team that lost possession

+ Progress to require players to only pass to members of their partner team

4V4V4 QUICK COMBINATIONS GAME

STAGES COVERED BY ACTIVITY
Stages 4 & 5 - 12-18 year old players

THEMES & COMPETENCIES
Theme:
+ Group defending.
+ Transition and attacking rhythm

Competencies:
+ Short and medium distance passing.
+ Receiving using different surfaces of the body.
+ Mobility on and off the ball.
+ Attacking in pairs and small groups.
+ Defending in pairs and small groups.

WHY USE IT
This game challenges players to focus on combination play, vision and quick transitions between offense and defense.

SET UP
A large playing area (approximately 30x40 yards). Divide players into 3 teams of 4, with the players from 1 team positioned with 1 player on each side.

HOW TO PLAY
2 interior teams play keep-away against each other inside the area. When a team completes 3 consecutive passes, that team can earn a point by playing the 4th pass to any target player on the outside edge. The team on the outside then enters the area, trading places with the players on the team that just scored.

COACHING NOTES
+ Coaching objectives – Look for players to be aware of their supporting options all around them (even behind them), and emphasize quick transition from defensive to attacking target roles.
+ Coaching tip – Although the game can be played in a square, a rectangular shape provides for some degree of orientation, similar to a regular game.
+ Adaptations – Add a requirement that the first pass after entering the area must be a long pass or a chip to a teammate on the other side of the area.

+ Players are free to dribble or pass anywhere inside the playing area
+ Target players can move anywhere along the edge of their border line

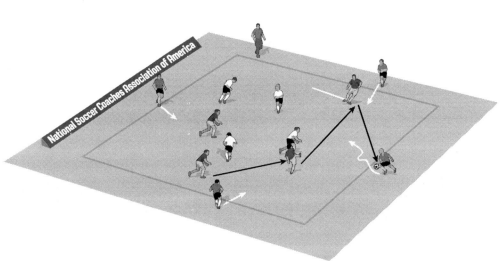

+ After completing 3 (or more) consecutive passes, the team scores by passing to any target player
+ The target players immediately enter the game as the scoring players replace them

+ You can increase the challenge by requiring a long pass to start each round

5V4 QUICK TRANSITIONS

STAGES COVERED BY ACTIVITY
Stages 3, 4 & 5 - 9-18 year old players

THEMES & COMPETENCIES
Theme:
+ Transition and attacking rhythm
+ Switching the point of attack
+ Counter attacking and finishing breakaways
+ Group defending.

Competencies:
+ Short and medium passing
+ Receiving using different surfaces of the body.
+ Mobility on and off the ball.
+ Attacking in pairs and small groups.
+ Defending in pairs and small groups.
+ Shooting technique

WHY USE IT
This fast-paced game trains players to counter-attack when they have a numerical advantage and to build the attack when they are at a disadvantage.

SET UP
55x45 yard field with 2 full-sized goals. A goalkeeper in each goal with a supply of balls. 2 teams in a line by its own goal.

HOW TO PLAY
5 players enter the playing area with a ball, challenged 4 players from the other team. If the ball crosses the sideline, the first player to retrieve the ball wins possession and restarts with a throw-in. If the ball crosses a goal line, the players defending that goal sprint off and are replaced by the same number of teammates. The new players coming on always start with the ball. Play for 8-10 minutes, then have the teams reverse roles to play a second half.

COACHING NOTES
+ Coaching objectives – Look for players to recognize numbers-up versus numbers-down situations, and choose between counter-attacking and build-up play accordingly.
+ Coaching tip – As a new team enters with the ball, remind them to avoid high-risk play in front of their own goal, and find ways to play the ball forward quickly.
+ Adaptations – Increase space and numbers.

+ Players from each team enter from the goal line to start each round.
+ Each team plays numbers-up for a half, then numbers-down for a half.

+ If the ball crosses the goal line for any reason, the group defending that end is replaced.
+ The new group brings in a new ball and plays away from the dangerous space near the goal.

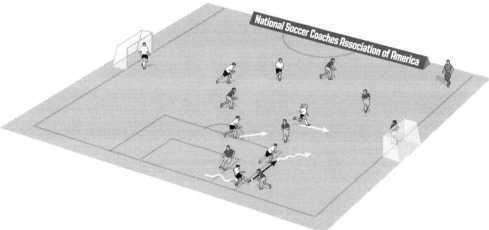

+ After half time the teams trade roles for the second half.
+ The team with the most total goals at the end of the full game wins.

STAGES COVERED BY ACTIVITY
Stages 4 & 5 - 12-18 year old players

THEMES & COMPETENCIES
Theme:
+ Transition and attacking rhythm
+ Switching the point of attack
+ Counter attacking and finishing breakaways
+ Group defending.

Competencies:
+ Short and medium passing
+ Receiving using different surfaces of the body.
+ Mobility on and off the ball.
+ Attacking in pairs and small groups.
+ Defending in pairs and small groups.
+ Shooting technique

WHY USE IT
This small-sided scrimmage allows you to assess whether your players are successfully implementing objectives under match conditions.

SET UP
70x55 yard area across one half of a full-size field. Divide your players into two teams (one wearing vests), and designate a goalkeeper for each team.

HOW TO PLAY
Play 7v7 to 2 full-size goals. Substitutions 'on the fly' (players may 'tag up' with a replacement player on the touchline at any time). All other laws as usual.

COACHING NOTES
+ Coaching objectives – Look for coordination of defensive effort across all tactical lines, from the goalkeeper to the forwards, and quick transition from defense to attack.
+ Coaching tip – Compared to an 11v11 scrimmage, the smaller-sided game offers players more touches and more opportunities to be engaged in the play, which increases the coach's chances to assess their technique and tactical understanding.
+ Adaptations – Give each team an opposing tactical situation (protecting/chasing a 1-goal lead, using/attacking a low line of confrontation, etc.) and play a 5-minute round before changing the scenario.

+ Defensively, the forwards work to reduce attacking options
+ Midfield players and defenders shift behind them to provide cover and balance

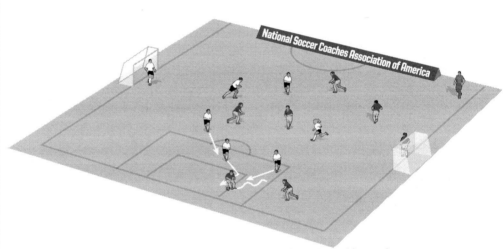

+ Forwards and Midfield players can work together to "double up" on wide attackers

+ When the defending team wins the ball, transition quickly to attack.

ATTACKING RHYTHM 3-ZONE GAME

STAGES COVERED BY ACTIVITY
Stages 4 & 5 - 12-18 year old players

THEMES & COMPETENCIES
Theme:
+ Transition and attacking rhythm
+ Switching the point of attack
+ Counter attacking and finishing breakaways
+ Group defending.

Competencies:
+ Short and medium passing
+ Receiving using different surfaces of the body.
+ Mobility on and off the ball.
+ Attacking in pairs and small groups.
+ Defending in pairs and small groups.
+ Shooting technique

WHY USE IT
This game requires players to adjust their collective attacking rhythm as they advance the ball through the thirds of the field.

SET UP
Set up a 70x55 yard field with a full-sized goal at each end, and use cones to divide the field into thirds (defensive, midfield, and attacking zones). 2 teams. Supply of extra balls available next to each goal.

HOW TO PLAY
8v8 (including Goalkeepers) with a 2-touch restriction in each defensive zone, 1-touch in the midfield zone, and unlimited touches in attacking zone.

COACHING NOTES
+ Coaching objectives – Focus on developing good awareness among all players regarding changes in the desired attacking rhythm as the ball moves through the thirds of the field.
+ Coaching tip – Call a 'thinking foul' whenever a player violates the required touch restriction, and award an indirect free kick to the other team from the spot of the 'foul'.
+ Adaptations – Change the touch restrictions in each zone.

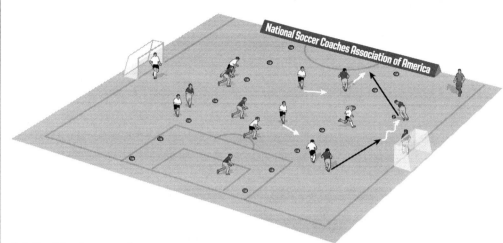

+ In the defensive zone, players use a touch to control the ball before passing with the second
+ Safety is the main concern in this part of the field

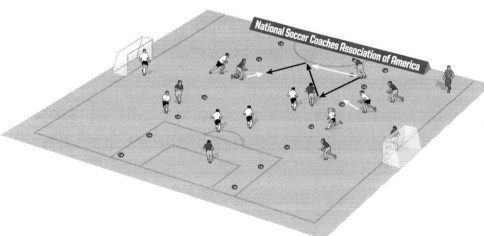

+ The game accelerates once the ball enters the midfield zone.
+ Supporting runs must come quickly in this area.

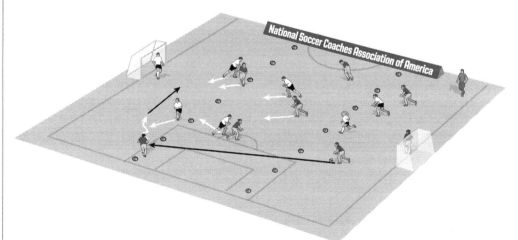

+ It is permissible to bypass the midfield with a long pass to a forward.
+ Forwards have the opportunity to attack with breakaways or combination play.

8V8 BUILD-UP ATTACKING GAME

STAGES COVERED BY ACTIVITY
Stages 4 & 5 - 12-18 year old players

THEMES & COMPETENCIES
Theme:
+ Transition and attacking rhythm
+ Switching the point of attack
+ Counter attacking and finishing breakaways
+ Group defending.

Competencies:
+ Short and medium passing
+ Receiving using different surfaces of the body.
+ Mobility on and off the ball.
+ Attacking in pairs and small groups.
+ Defending in pairs and small groups.
+ Shooting technique

WHY USE IT
This game encourages players to maintain ball possession looking for opportunities to break through a compact defense.

SET UP
70x55 yard field with 2 full-sized goals. Use cones to mark a halfway line. 2 teams of 8 (7v7 plus two goalkeepers).

HOW TO PLAY
Play a regular game of soccer with 3 restrictions: 1) All players may go forward into the attacking half, but no more than 5 field players may drop back into a team's defensive zone; 2) Teams can score points by either scoring a goal or by completing 10 consecutive passes made entirely in the attacking half of the field; 3) Goalkeepers must distribute the ball to a teammate who receives the ball in the defensive half of the field. Enforce the offside law. The team with the most points when time expires wins the game.

COACHING NOTES
+ Coaching objectives – Look for players to recognize when there are opportunities to go to goal, and to be disciplined in possession.
+ Coaching tip – Require players to count passes out loud in the attacking half to reinforce this aspect of the game.
+ Adaptations – Increase the attacking difficulty by allowing all but one player to drop back into the defensive half.

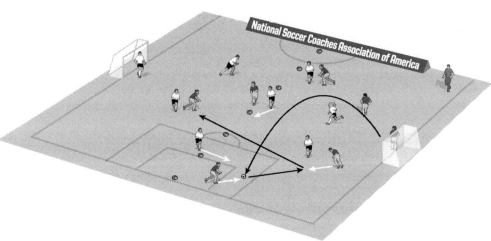

+ Goalkeeper distribution must be played to a teammate in the defensive half.
+ The team then works the ball quickly out of the back into the attacking half.

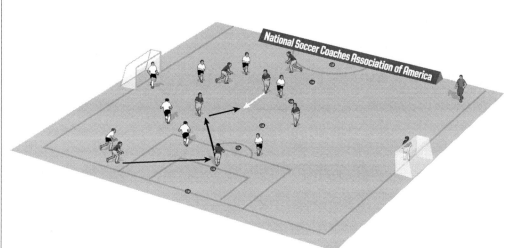

+ When the defense is well-organized, the attackers pass the ball to keep possession
+ 10 consecutive passes in the attacking half earns a point, and the opponent then restarts with the ball

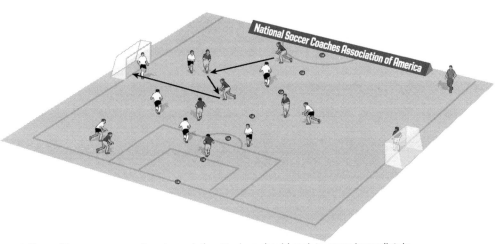

+ If a probing pass opens a lane to goal, the attackers should seek to score immediately.

STAGE 5: PLAYERS 15-18 YEARS OLD

STAGE 5 - ADOLESCENCE: LATE PUBERTY/EARLY ADULTHOOD (15-18 YEARS OLD)

During middle adolescence, puberty is well underway, and is complete in many teenagers. There is a decreased preoccupation with the body and an increased involvement with peers. Parental conflicts develop over independence, since the peer group often serves as the adolescent's reference for their standards of behavior. By the age of 16, most girls have completed the changes associated with puberty and most boys are well on their way to finishing pubertal development, having gained muscle mass and strength. If players in stage five have received appropriate coaching in stages 1-4, they will be ready to perform competently in game situations.

DEVELOPMENT FOCUS

- Team tactics should form a significant part of practice sessions and teams should be coached in team 'units' – defense, midfield and attack.
- Position training is important, and players should be prepared for a primary position.
- Physical conditioning is also important for all players and training should be tailored to the physical demands of their position on the field.
- On average, boys reach PHV in Stage 5. Aerobic power should be introduced progressively after growth rate decelerates.
- Optimum time for the introduction of strength training for boys (1-1 ½ years following PHV)
- The second speed training window opens for boys (13-16 years)
- Participation in other sports can enhance physical preparation and transferability to soccer. However, soccer should be the primary sport for serious and committed players.

KEY DEVELOPMENT POINTS FOR CHILDREN IN STAGE 5

Physically	Psychological/Social	Cognitive/Mental
1. Start of speed and strength training for male and female players.	1. Increased interest in the opposite sex.	1. More defined work habits
2. Aerobic conditioning following peak height velocity.	2. Decreased conflict with parents.	2. More concern about future educational and vocational plans
3. Girls reach full maturity at the beginning of Stage 5 and boys peak around 16 years of age.	3. Deeper capacity for caring and sharing, and the development of more intimate relationships.	3. Greater ability to sense right and wrong
4. Shows improved posture and coordination in coping with physical changes.	4. Decrease time spent with parents and more time spent with peers.	4. Sadness or depression, which can lead to poor grades at school, alcohol or drug abuse, unsafe sex, thoughts of suicide, and other problems (Note: Problems at school, alcohol and drug abuse, and other disorders can also lead to feelings of sadness or hopelessness.)
5. Needs to continue fitness activities, especially those that develop flexibility, aerobic and anaerobic efficiency, muscular strength and endurance.	5. Strong social needs and desires.	
	6. Wants and needs own voice in planning.	
	7. Desires leadership roles.	5. Able to learn new skills in a short time.
6. Can achieve advanced levels of complex skill and movement efficiency.	8. Team and group allegiance important.	6. Thinking becomes more practical and adaptive to take into account logical reasoning.
7. Decreases in flexibility.	9. Developing into an independent person who is increasingly able to make choices, solve problems and accept responsibility for own actions.	7. Changes are multi-directional and depend on education and understanding of the world.
	10. Developing more stable and emotional responses.	

DEVELOPMENT CHARACTERISTICS TRANSLATED TO COACHING PLAYERS IN STAGE 5

At Stage 5, the players should have a firm grounding in all basic skills, techniques, movement skills, tactics and strategies. Depending on the individual's level of performance and understanding, coaches can progress to advanced tactics. Players should play to win, but training should still emphasize skill, physical and mental development. After players reach peak height velocity (the point when the tempo of growth is the greatest), aerobic training should be emphasized and conducted as much as possible with the ball at the players feet. Stage 5 also represents a window of opportunity for training speed. Gender differences exist; with second window opening for females with the onset of menarche (first menstrual period). For males, there is only one window and it begins a year to 18 months after peak height velocity.

TRANSLATED TO PLAYER DEVELOPMENT THIS MEANS

1. Start of speed and strength training for male and female players (see above for timing).
2. Aerobic conditioning following peak height velocity.
3. Mental skills training to cope with stressful situations and mental challenges of competition.
4. Elite players should be focusing on soccer as the primary activity and supplemented by one other sport.
5. Training ratios should be 60:40 to competitive games.
6. Latest developments in sports science research should be reviewed and where applicable adopted.
7. Balanced strength training should be adopted – ensuring all muscles are equally trained.
8. Players should train in competitive situations in the form of practice matches and phases of play.
9. Players should be encouraged to watch high level games (college, WPS, MLS etc) to help understand advanced tactics and strategies.
10. Monitor over-training of players – ensure sufficient rest for recovery.
11. Nutritional and fluid intake advice should be sought.
12. Establish winning as a major objective of participation.
13. Involve players in decision making.
14. Use goal setting to provide direction and performance targets
15. Utilize different training methods such as video analysis, classroom discussions and team building.
16. Players should be challenged continuously – physically and mentally.
17. Warm-up and flexibility routines are extremely important before and after a training session or game.
18. Players should start to play one positional role more regularly – this may include playing different midfield positions for example.
19. Ensure good two-way communication exists; do not allow hormones to be an excuse for negative or bad behavior.
20. Be conscious of favoring early maturing over late maturing players.

5V5 FUNCTIONING AS 5V3

STAGES COVERED BY ACTIVITY
Stages 3, 4 & 5 - 9-18 year old players

THEMES & COMPETENCIES
Theme:
+ Group and team defending.
+ Team possession and purpose.

Competencies:
+ Defending in small groups - applying pressure, covering and support.
+ Transition from defense to attack and attack to defense.
+ Passing a short and medium distance.
+ Receiving a pass.
+ Attacking in small groups.

WHY USE IT
This exercise is a terrific way of teaching players high pressure defending roles (1st, 2nd, 3rd), coordination and also transition into possession.

SET UP
Utilize a 20x20 yard grid divided in half with a line of cones as shown. The coach is stationed at the side of the grid with a ball supply for all re-starts.

HOW TO PLAY
The exercise begins with the coach playing a ball into one team. The ball is immediately passed to the other team (simulating a turnover). The defending team send 3 players into their opponent's half of the grid to try to win back the ball. When the ball is won it is passed or dribbled back into the other half of the grid and the 2 teams change roles. Look to see if players understand first (pressure, make play predictable), second (cover) and third (balance) defender roles and how to interchange.

COACHING NOTES
+ Main coaching objectives – Can the defending players get in and establish immediate pressure?
+ Coaching Tip - Stop the action to adjust defending positions, careful to emphasize angles and distances.
+ Adaptations: Serves from grid to grid must be in the air; expand or shrink the grid to adjust pressure.

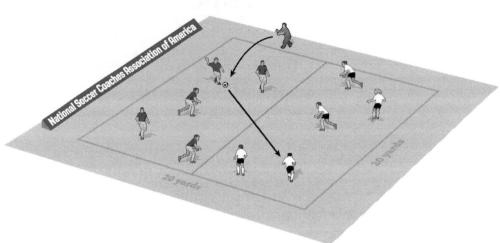

+ Coach plays into one team and the ball is served to the opponent.

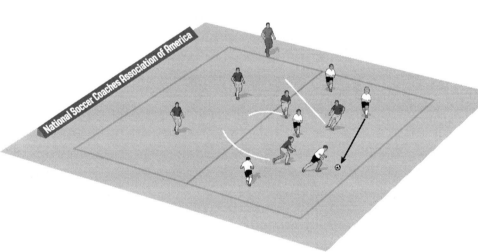

+ Players from the defending team get into the opponent's zone
+ 1st player looks to pressure while 2 and 3 cover.
+ Meanwhile, the white team combine passes

+ The pressurizing run forces the ball to be played back
+ The cover and balance defenders have read the options available
+ Cover defender wins the ball and plays it back into the blue team's grid.

IMPRINTING ZONAL DEFENDING 4V4

STAGES COVERED BY ACTIVITY
Stages 4 & 5 - 12-18 year old players

THEMES & COMPETENCIES
Theme:
+ Group and team defending.

Competencies:
+ Defending as a unit - applying pressure, covering and support.
+ Transition from defense to attack and attack to defense.
+ Passing a short and medium distance.
+ Receiving a pass.
+ Attacking in small groups.

WHY USE IT
This is a terrific environment for training shape, communication, recognition and collective movement to teach zonal defending on the back and/or midfield lines.

SET UP
Use a 20x20 yard grid to start. Expand as needed. Note the cone line down the center.

HOW TO PLAY
The coach initiates the action by passing to either team. The receiving team slowly work the ball back and forth (square) across the grid, pausing after each pass to allow the defending team to set their zonal shape. In this phase, the defenders are not allowed to challenge for the ball. After each team has mastered the interchanges, allow the 2 teams to challenge each other for possession while keeping their shapes. The coach needs to spend considerable time with the group emphasizing the key components of zonal defending.

COACHING NOTES
+ Main coaching objectives – Note the overall shape (hook or J), the first, second and third defender roles and how they interchange, and also the variables (i.e. do you want your team to force the ball inside or outside?)
+ Coaching Tip - Players in a zone must dress their positions off one another to assure the zone shape is correct. Therefore, they must look to their left and right with every movement.
+ Adaptations - The cone line is a nice added touch in that it serves as a restraining line, or point at which the team will try to win back the ball. Add corner goals (2 for each team to play to), a pair of defenders and a single striker.

+ The coach plays the ball in to the blue team.
+ Players make passes back and forth across the field.
+ The defending team attempt to set their zone with each pass.

+ The zone is set when the ball is in the opponents possession and in a central position.
+ Defenders attempt to force the ball centrally.

+ Each team now fields a pair of defenders and a forward in addition to the midfield group.
+ Add corner goals.

PRESSING, LOW AND HIGH PRESSURE

STAGES COVERED BY ACTIVITY
Stages 4 & 5 - 12-18 year old players

THEMES & COMPETENCIES
Theme:
+ Group and team defending.

Competencies:
+ Defending as a unit and team - applying pressure, covering and support.
+ Transition from defense to attack and attack to defense.

WHY USE IT
Applying varied defending styles in the match allows the coach to adjust the team's posture to various game situations, opponents and conditions.

SET UP
Full field to full-sized goals.

HOW TO PLAY
11v11 game. Work with one team at a time. Many teams assume that applying high pressure simply involves more energy is expended further up the field trying to win back the ball. The target team should learn to press the opponent in a high pressure mind-frame (see cues below) and then also to play low pressure. As the teams become accustomed to varying their approach over several sessions, play one style against the other and then have them change styles within the game.

COACHING NOTES
+ Main coaching objectives – Pressing is a systematic effort to limit an opponent's options and space in possession and thereby produce turnovers. The roles of every player on the field in this design must be rehearsed and well-understood.
+ Coaching Tip - Ask players when the team might employ high or low pressure in a match setting. It is important they understand the reasons why the team would adopt a certain posture.
+ Adaptations - Award a point for each time a team wins the ball after successfully adopting a given posture.

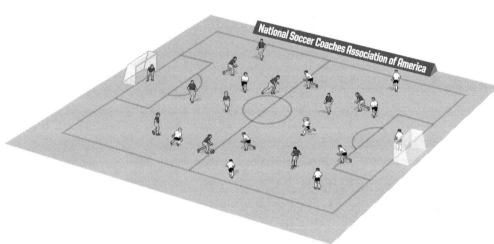

+ 11v11 game free play to begin.

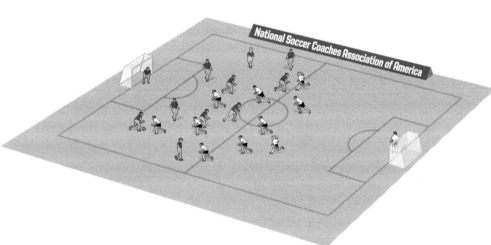

+ High pressure - the forward in the defending team's 4-2-3-1 is attempting to force the ball forward.
+ The remainder of the team fills in behind to force play in front of the player in possession.

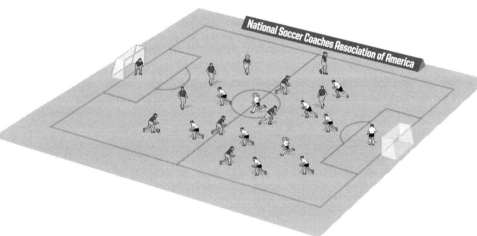

+ The defending team now plays low pressure
+ A restraining line is set at mid field.
+ Back line is deep to prevent a ball being played in behind.

COUNTER-STRIKE 3V3

STAGES COVERED BY ACTIVITY
Stages 3, 4 & 5 - 9-18 year old players

THEMES & COMPETENCIES
Theme:
+ Team possession with purpose.
+ Group and team defending.

Competencies:
+ Transition from defense to attack and attack to defense.
+ Passing a short and medium distance.
+ Receiving a pass.
+ Attacking in small groups.
+ Defending as a unit and team - applying pressure, covering and support.

WHY USE IT
This exercise teaches players to recognize the moment to counter and get numbers into the attack.

SET UP
24x18 yard field divided in half and featuring small goals at each end.

HOW TO PLAY
2 teams of 3. Each team plays 2 defenders (in the back half) and an attacker (in the front half) of the grid. Players are confined to their zones and goals can only be scored from the front half of the grid. Firstly, the player in the defending half who passes in to the target player in the front half must join that player and can remain there until a goal is scored or possession is lost. Secondly, when one player from the defensive zone passes in to the target, the other player in the defensive zone must go forward in support of the ball.

COACHING NOTES
+ Main coaching objectives – The ability of the attacking player to post up and hold the ball against a defender(s), and combination play are important coaching points.
+ Coaching Tip - Do your players attempt to change speed in attack? Counter-attacking is about rhythm and all players need to adapt to the need for faster play as the team moves forward.
+ Adaptations - Play 2 games on adjacent fields. Add a goalkeeper on each end. The goalkeepers must move back and forth from one field to the other and join the play.

+ 3v3 to small goals.
+ 2v1 in each end.

+ Player passing in to the target player must immediately run forward in support of the attack.

+ The player off the ball must get forward in support of the attack when his partner plays into the target player.

11V11 TO MULTIPLE GOALS

STAGES COVERED BY ACTIVITY
Stages 4 & 5 - 12-18 year old players

THEMES & COMPETENCIES
Theme:
+ Team possession with purpose.
+ Group and team defending.

Competencies:
+ Transition from defense to attack and attack to defense.
+ Passing short, medium and long distances.
+ Defending as a unit and team - applying pressure, covering and support.

WHY USE IT
This exercise takes the principles of counter-attacking to the full game, allowing players to learn patterns useful to countering under pressure on match day.

SET UP
Two full teams 11v11 on a full field with full-sized goals and four small wide channel goals - two for each team.

HOW TO PLAY
Begin by playing a standard scrimmage for a few minutes to let the players settle into the game. Then explain to players that they can earn 3 points for scoring off a counter-attack and an additional point for dribbling or passing through either of the channel goals on either side in their front half of the field. Counters do not need to go through these areas (a central goal can be added as well), but the chance for an added point gets players to think about where to put the ball early in a counter-attacking situation.

COACHING NOTES
+ Main coaching objectives – This game encourages players to get the ball forward early when the ball is won. Wide goals represent areas often useful for building counter-attacks.
+ Coaching Tip - Stop the action and ask the players if they made the right choice based on the shape of the team, time of game, etc.
+ Adaptations - Some coaches like to put time limits or incentives on a counter as well to emphasize speed in the attack.

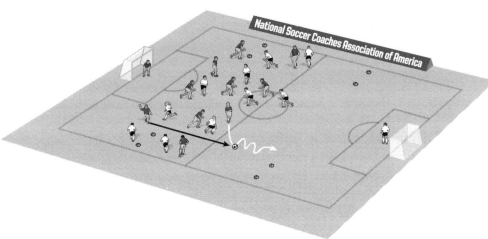

+ 11v11 game with channel goals and emphasis on counter-attacking.
+ A quick counter over the top with a striker getting in on goal.

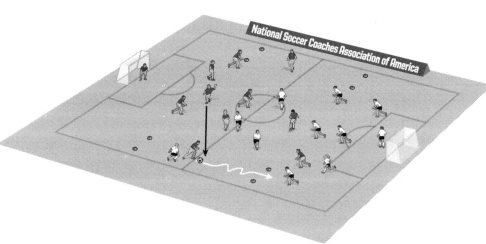

+ Long ball forward is not on when the ball is won.
+ The center back plays a wide midfielder who dribbles through the wide channel for a point.

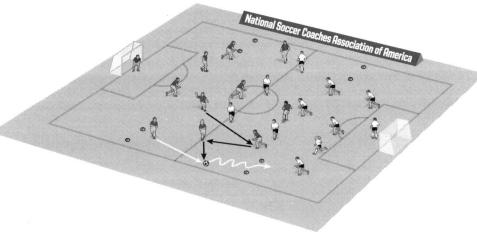

+ Long service into the striker to start the counter.
+ Ball is laid off to a holding midfielder
+ Near-side forward has run central to open the channel for the defender's run

TWO-BALL TECHNICAL TRAINING

STAGES COVERED BY ACTIVITY
Stages 3, 4 & 5 - 9-18 year old players

THEMES & COMPETENCIES
Theme:
+ Advanced technical training and fitness.

Competencies:
+ Receiving - foot, thigh, chest and head.
+ Short passing - speed of play.
+ Anaerobic endurance training.
+ Individual receiving and passing technique.

WHY USE IT
This advanced technical training environment is an efficient means of training skill in a pressure setting. The resting players still get plenty of touches, particularly in the first phase, and play is fast and challenging.

SET UP
Groups of 4. 2 balls per group. 3 players in an arc serve to 1 working player.

HOW TO PLAY
One server passes to the working player, who passes first-time to the open player. The other server who had a ball at the start then passes to the working player who again finds the open player and play continues. This is a pressure training exercise. The working player should be compelled to play at the very edge of his or her ability to pass with quality. Serves must come immediately one after another.

COACHING NOTES
+ Main coaching objectives – Is the player using the proper foot, based on the target player to be passed to?
+ Coaching Tip - Challenge the servers to work as hard as the working player. Their timing makes the exercise work at peak efficiency.
+ Adaptations - 1) Servers toss balls for the working player to volley to the open target. 2) Players toss balls for the working player to head to the open target.

+ One server plays into the feet of the working player
+ Working player plays to the open server.

+ A server tosses the ball to the working player, who volleys to the open server.

+ Servers toss to the working player's head for a first-time return to the open server.

WINDOWS FITNESS

STAGES COVERED BY ACTIVITY
Stages 3, 4 & 5 - 9-18 year old players

THEMES & COMPETENCIES
Theme:
+ Advanced technical training and fitness.

Competencies:
+ Receiving - foot, thigh, chest and head.
+ Short passing - speed of play.
+ Anaerobic endurance training.
+ Individual receiving and passing technique.

WHY USE IT
This exercise is a flexible, efficient environment for combining fitness and technical training.

SET UP
The area used varies with the number of players and the need to balance the number of touches with the fitness component. A larger grid will expand the fitness component but limit the number of touches and exchanges with the perimeter players - 2 squares, 25x25 yard square with a 5x5 yard square in the center.

HOW TO PLAY
Divide the team in 2 equal teams. One team, each with soccer balls, begins in the center grid. The other group forms a perimeter. The central players dribble out of the grid to within 5 yards of a perimeter player and pass the ball. They must then turn and run through the grid and receive a ball from any other perimeter player. One minute and then rotate the groups. Progressions can include keeping the balls with the perimeter players, who serve a ball to players running out of the grid. The active player can volley/settle/head back to the server.

COACHING NOTES
+ Objectives: Active players must play at speed throughout. Can they perform at a high technical level as they tire?
+ Tip: Expand or shrink the central grid (or use multiple grids or gates) to vary the fitness component or add a specific dribbling requirement (i.e. laces touches only).
+ Adaptations: Vary the exchange with the perimeter player to a combination (1-2, or overlap).

+ Basic set-up for the exercise with working players and servers ready to play.

+ Active players dribble to within 5 yards of perimeter targets.
+ Pass and run back through the central grid.

+ Variation with flagged central grid and gates in front of each server.
+ Active players run through gate, volley back to server and turn and run through central grid.

TECHNICAL SPEED SHORT 4'S

STAGES COVERED BY ACTIVITY
Stages 3, 4 & 5 - 9-18 year old players

THEMES & COMPETENCIES
Theme:
+ Advanced technical training and fitness.

Competencies:
+ Receiving - foot, thigh, chest and head.
+ Short passing - speed of play.
+ Anaerobic endurance training.
+ Individual receiving and passing technique.

WHY USE IT
This is an advanced exercise that provides both physical and technical pressure and also has many useful variations.

SET UP
12x12 yard area with a 3 yard cone gate and flag as shown.

HOW TO PLAY
In the base exercise players dribble at speed through the center gate and leave the ball for the first player in the opposing line. Players must sprint off the ball. Subsequent variations vary - dribbling and add back-pedalling and/ or a run around the flag. Another great variation: With a ball supply at one line, serve balls in the air for a player from the other line to pass, volley or head back before running around the flag. The server then sprints to the other line. Note the coach in the foreground with a ball supply in case the ball leaves the area. Play for one minute and then rest before trying variations.

COACHING NOTES
+ Objectives: Can the players work at speed while still being sharp on the ball even as fatigue starts to set in?
+ Coaching Tip: Think of alternatives to using a flag; such as hurdles, agility ladders, a medicine ball to throw, all give great extra physical training.
+ Adaptations There are many additional useful variations. For instance, vary the type of dribbling (laces, one touch for every step, specific dribbling patterns).

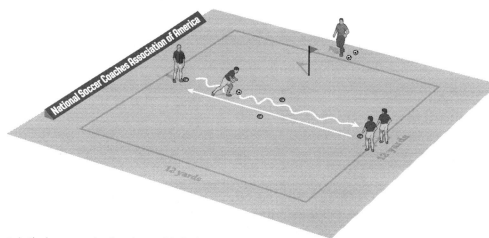

+ In the base exercise the player with the ball dribbles at speed to the opposite line.
+ Leave the ball for the next player
+ Then attempt to sprint back before the next dribbler can get there.

+ Dribble at speed to the gate
+ Pass to the first player in the opposite line
+ Back-pedal at speed to own line.

+ Dribbler goes at speed to the gate.
+ Pass and sprint around the flag and join the other line.

FITNESS LONG PASSING

STAGES COVERED BY ACTIVITY
Stages 4 & 5 - 12-18 year old players

THEMES & COMPETENCIES
Theme:
+ Advanced technical training and fitness.

Competencies:
+ Receiving - foot, thigh, chest and head.
+ Medium and long distance passing.
+ Anaerobic endurance training.
+ Individual receiving and passing technique.

WHY USE IT
A great way to mix long passing and fitness work. The ability to play over distance on tired legs is a very good technical test.

SET UP
Groups of 5 playing in and between two 12x12 yard grids (twenty-five yards between grids).

HOW TO PLAY
3 players pass the ball against a single defender who can only play at half-speed to start. If the defender wins the ball, play restarts immediately with no role changes. The attackers must complete 2 passes (or more) and then play a long pass to the other grid, where the 5th player awaits. When the long pass is played, the player making the long pass remains in the grid, while the other 3 players (2 attackers and the defender) sprint to the other grid. The last player to arrive is the new defender. Play for 3 minutes and then rest before playing again.

COACHING NOTES
+ Objectives: Can players serve under pressure on tired legs and then make long runs in support of the ball after a change of fields?
+ Coaching Tip: Watch the activity closely and create balanced groups to ensure the work load is evenly shared.
+ Adaptations: All serves must be with the non-preferred foot; all play is with the non-preferred foot; defending player gives full effort.

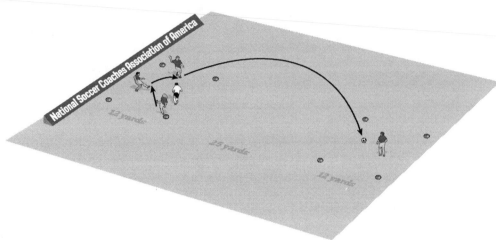

+ Attackers pass twice and play a long pass to the target in the far grid.
+ Defender starts at ½ pace.

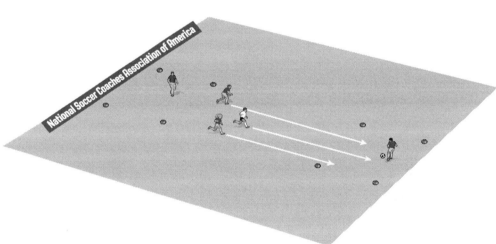

+ The player passing long remains in the grid while the other 3 players race to the other grid.

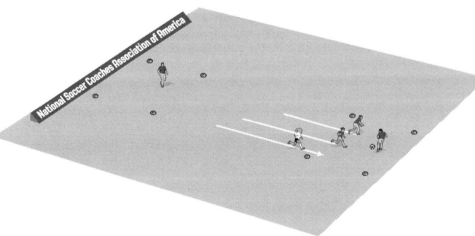

+ The first two players to arrive in the grid join the player in possession.
+ Last player to arrive becomes the new defender and play continues.

WHIRLPOOL AND STEEPLE CHASE

STAGES COVERED BY ACTIVITY
Stages 4 & 5 - 12-18 year old players

THEMES & COMPETENCIES
Theme:
+ Advanced technical training and fitness.

Competencies:
+ Anaerobic endurance training.

WHY USE IT
These two exercises are easy to set up - very demanding soccer fitness environments.

SET UP
Whirlpool – 25x25 yard grid; Steeple Chase – 3x30 yard area.

HOW TO PLAY
Whirlpool - Divide the team into 3 equal groups. Each group starts at a corner (leave one open) of the grid. Groups run clock-wise around the perimeter of the grid. The first group runs until they reach the next group and then stops. Run for 3 minutes and then rest before continuing. Steeple Chase - Similar except that players are grouped in pairs or threes at cones laid out in a circle. Each group runs 2 cones and then stops. Note that the first 2 stations have extra players to keep the exercise going when the exercise circles around.

COACHING NOTES
+ Objectives: Both of these exercises provide soccer-specific fitness training with short, sharp sprints and minimal rest. Who can win each group run? Are those who win the early runs able to sustain their superiority as they tire?
+ Coaching Tip: Each group must wait for the first member of the previous group to arrive before starting his or her run. No one can cut corners.
+ Adaptations: Run with a soccer ball. Vary the distances. At a signal runners change directions. For a cool-down players must juggle from one station to the next.

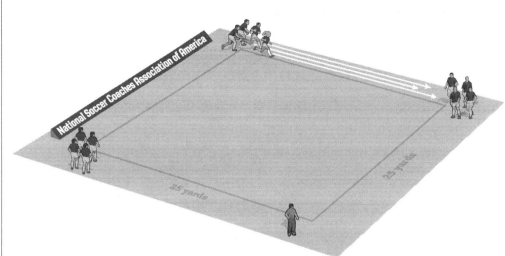

+ Whirlpool - Base exercise with groups running clock-wise until they reach the next group.

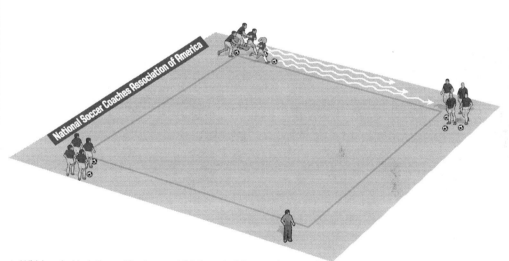

+ Whirlpool - Variation with players dribbling a ball from point-to-point.

+ Steeple chase - Players run in pairs, sprinting past the first cone and onto the second cone before stopping.

DUTCH PASSING PATTERNS

STAGES COVERED BY ACTIVITY
Stages 3, 4 & 5 - 9-18 year old players

THEMES & COMPETENCIES
Theme:
+ Advanced technical training and fitness.
+ Team possession with purpose.

Competencies:
+ Anaerobic endurance training.
+ Receiving with feet.
+ Passing over short and medium distances.
+ Passing techniques - chip, lofted, driven and swerve.
+ Mental conditioning - decision making and speed of play.
+ Support with and without the ball.

WHY USE IT
Teach players to play with refined technique at speed and think in terms of pattern play.

SET UP
12x20 to a 20x20 yard grid. 5 players – 1 player starts in each corner and a target player starts in the center.

HOW TO PLAY
Player 1 passes along the side line to player 2. Player 2 opens his/her body, receives and passes in 2 touches to the target player 3 in the center. Player 3 must check away and then meet the ball. Player 3 turns and passes to either corner at the other end of the grid. Critically, player 3 runs in the other direction from the pass. Seeing the target player running towards him/ her, the corner player now exchanges position and becomes a new center player. As the exchange occurs the player receiving the pass from the target player passes along the sideline to the other corner player. Now the pattern repeated.

COACHING NOTES
+ Objectives: How quickly can the players work while still playing with proper technique?
+ Tip: Which foot is correct to play a pass to the target? Playing with and to the correct foot adds speed.
+ Adaptations: Add a second target player. Target players split to create space and the pass from the end line is to the furthest player.

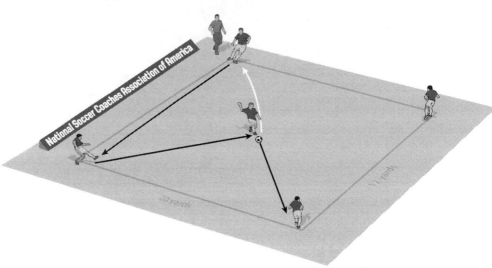

+ Start with a pass along end line and a second pass to the checking target player.
+ Work with the target to turn with minimal touches and use different moves and body positions.
+ The target passes to far end of grid before changing positions in the opposite direction.

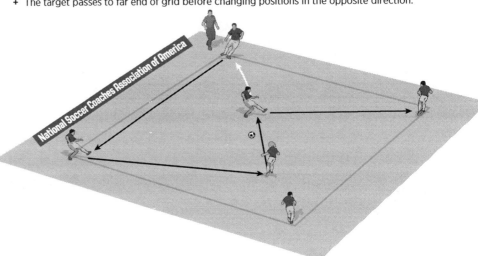

+ Add a second central player
+ Note the extra pass and the rotation pattern - ball played to furthest target first and lay off.
+ The central player passing the ball rotates changes and the other player stays.

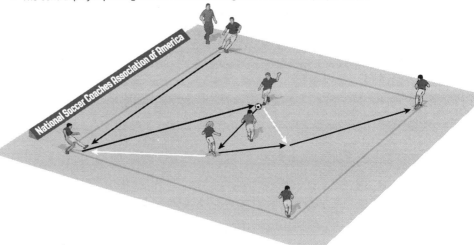

+ Add a central, passive defender and change defender every couple of minutes
+ The central players play around the defender and use a 1-2 to beat the defender.

STAGES COVERED BY ACTIVITY
Stages 3, 4 & 5 - 9-18 year old players

THEMES & COMPETENCIES
Theme:
+ Advanced technical training and fitness.
+ Team possession with purpose.
+ Group and team defending.

Competencies:
+ Anaerobic endurance training.
+ Receiving with feet.
+ Passing over short and medium distances.
+ Passing techniques - chip, lofted, driven and swerve.
+ Mental conditioning - decision making and speed of play.
+ Support with and without the ball.
+ Pressure, cover and support.

WHY USE IT
Fun, challenging and intense warm-up for possession theme.

SET UP
Start with 30x30 yards for teams of 16-18 players. 3 soccer balls (2 of one color and one of another). Two equal teams.

HOW TO PLAY
One team has a ball and passes the ball with their feet only, counting passes as they go. If they get to 15 passes, they earn a point. The other team has 2 'spike' balls that can only be moved by throwing to one-another (allow only 3 running steps in possession). They must attempt to pass the ball between their teammates so they can throw a 'Spiker' and hit the other team's ball to earn the point. First team to 3 points wins.

COACHING NOTES
+ Objectives: Both teams have training targets. The possession team must know where the Spikers are and avoid them while quickly passing. The Spikers must coordinate their efforts to destroy their opponent's possession.
+ Coaching Tip: Adjust the size of the grid to increase or decrease the pressure on the possession team.
+ Adaptations: Require a combination/s as part of the possession team's sequence - i.e. An overlap.

+ White team pass the ball with feet to achieve 15 passes
+ Blue team use their hands to move their two balls close enough to 'spike.'
+ Blue player in possession is only allowed 3 steps.

+ White team players pass the ball between them aiming for 15 passes.
+ Blue player throws to teammate who 'spikes' the ball as white player attempts to pass to – 1 point to the blue team!

+ White players complete a required overlap for a point while avoiding the blue 'spikers'.

CONE DROP - SOPHISTICATED POSSESSION GAME

STAGES COVERED BY ACTIVITY
Stages 3, 4 & 5 - 9-18 year old players

THEMES & COMPETENCIES
Theme:
+ Advanced technical training.
+ Team possession with purpose.
+ Group and team defending.

Competencies:
+ Receiving.
+ Passing over short and medium distances.
+ Passing techniques - chip, lofted, driven and swerve.
+ Mental conditioning - decision making and speed of play.
+ Support with and without the ball.
+ Pressure, cover and support.

WHY USE IT
This is an activity observed during a professional team training session in Germany. A possession game where players must think as well as play.

SET UP
35x35 yard grid. 3 teams of 5-6 players in 3 colors. Players in 1 team spread out and hold 2 cones corresponding to the colors of the other team's vests – 1 in each hand.

HOW TO PLAY
This is a possession game where the 2 active teams (without cones) try to possess the ball and those holding cones are playing in support of the team in possession. When a member of the stationary team receives a pass from another team, they must pass back to a player in the same team. The stationary player cannot be tackled. Once a pass is made, the stationary player drops the cone corresponding to that team's color. The first team to have all of the cones of their color dropped wins.

COACHING NOTES
+ Objectives: Quick passing can lead to quick points.
+ Coaching Tip: Encourage target players to continue to call for the ball even after they have dropped all cones of a color. If they receive a pass, they pick up the cone of the color that passed to them!
+ Adaptations: The inactive team can move throughout the grid. Add a goalkeeper and any serve caught by the goalkeeper is worth a point.

+ Blue team players hold cones corresponding to the color of the other teams vests.
+ White and red play a possession game.
+ The team in possession attempt to pass to blue players that are holding the cone corresponding to their team's color vest..

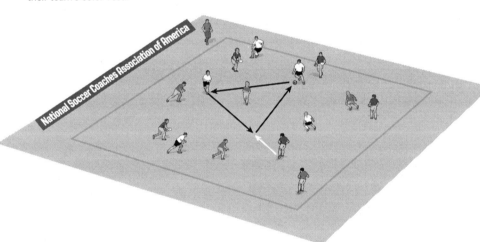

+ Blue players can now move.
+ White players combine passes with a blue target checking to the ball.

+ Add goalkeeper playing for the team in possession
+ White team combine passes and play to the goalkeeper's hands for a point.

MANY GOALS

STAGES COVERED BY ACTIVITY
Stages 4 & 5 - 12-18 year old players

THEMES & COMPETENCIES
Theme:
+ Advanced technical training.
+ Team possession with purpose.
+ Group and team defending.

Competencies:
+ Receiving.
+ Passing over short and medium distances.
+ Passing techniques - chip, lofted, driven and swerve.
+ Mental conditioning - decision making and speed of play.
+ Support with and without the ball.
+ Pressure, cover and support.

WHY USE IT
Flexible, functional exercise that can be used to coax a team to play through target areas or learn to probe an opponent in possession.

SET UP
For advanced teams use a full field and two full teams. Field size can be adjusted to accommodate smaller numbers.

HOW TO PLAY
This is a standard scrimmage with the 2 teams playing to goal. The coach can tweak the setup to encourage players to switch fields, play wide in the various thirds, or with a series of random goals throughout the field probe an opponent. Diagram 1: the team finds a runner through a gate (not necessary to play the ball through the gate). Diagram 2: shows a pair of cone goals to play or run through. This encourages width and wide attacking in the final third. Diagram 3: many goals to encourage the teams to probe their opponents in possession. 1 point for playing through any gate and 3 for a goal.

COACHING NOTES
+ Objectives: Typically, goals compel or encourage players to think of rewards for utilizing a particular or varied approach to build-up.
+ Coaching Tip: Require a particular combination before playing through a goal(s).
+ Adaptations: Move cone goals vertically and horizontally to adjust the team's focus and tactics.

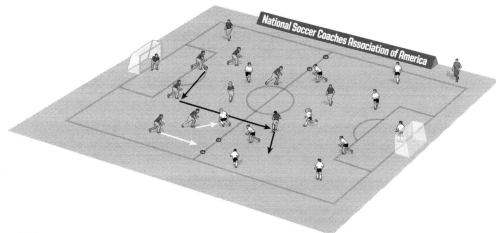

+ Wide goals.
+ The team in possession build up by pinching the right flank player and overlapping the right back through the gate into the attack.

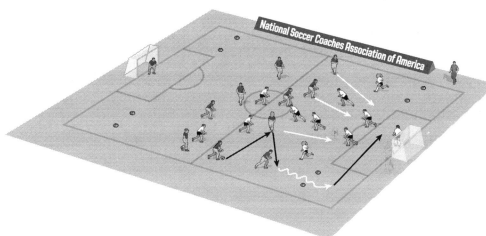

+ Wide goal channels in the front third for each team.
+ The attackers use a combination to release the right midfielder to dribble to the end line to cross.

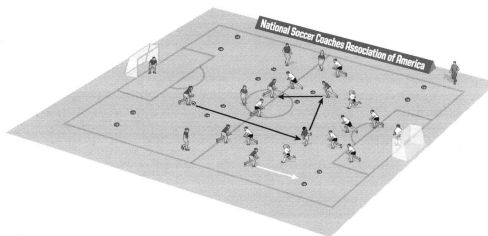

+ Many goals.
+ Team in possession play through a gate to their target, but the opposition is defending the flank well.
+ The target finds the attacking midfielder who lays off through another gate to a holding midfielder.

STAGES COVERED BY ACTIVITY
Stages 4 & 5 - 12-18 year old players

THEMES & COMPETENCIES
Theme:
+ Team possession with purpose.
+ Group and team defending.

Competencies:
+ Receiving.
+ Passing over short and medium distances.
+ Passing techniques - chip, lofted, driven and swerve.
+ Mobility on and off the ball.
+ Mental conditioning - decision making and speed of play.
+ Support with and without the ball.
+ Pressure, cover and support.

WHY USE IT
This is perhaps the best functional and highly-structured model for developing build-up play.

SET UP
For advanced players, utilize a full field and two full teams.

HOW TO PLAY
This activity follows the possession activities previously presented and the rules are a standard scrimmage. The main variation is that players are confined to start in one of 3 thirds of the field. The format can be used with 8v8-11v11 systems. In this 11v11, both teams have 4 defenders in the defending third - 5 midfield players in the middle third - and a forward in the attacking third. A coach can certainly change the formation and even play different formations for each team. To start, a player can only enter a more attacking zone if he/she passes into the next third and then follows the pass. When possession is lost players must recover to their original zone.

COACHING NOTES
+ Objectives: Teach players the value of creating overloads in areas of the field.
+ Coaching Tip: Emphasize the odds in each third (i.e. 4v1 in the back) in encouraging players to think about forward mobility!
+ Adaptations: When a player passes forward into the next third, he/she and one more player can move forward in support. This teaches players to run off the ball.

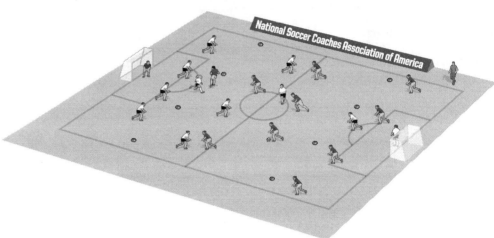

+ 2 teams set up in similar formations 1-4-5-1 in the thirds of the field.
+ Mobility is a key concept and players should look to create overloads.
+ Passes can be made laterally and back to a player in space.

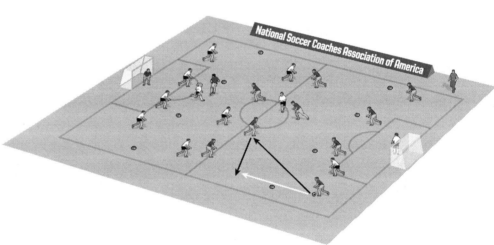

+ Creating an overload in the midfield build-up.
+ Blue left back plays into the midfield and follows his pass.
+ Forward player starts a run across the field to support.

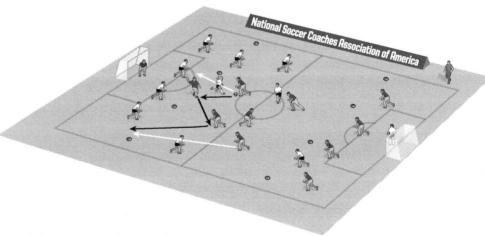

+ 2 players are allowed to support in the next zone
+ The Blue midfielder plays into the feet of the target player and follows the pass.
+ Another Blue midfielder makes a blindside run up the flank off the ball.

CROSS AND RECYCLE: TIMING AND EFFICIENCY

STAGES COVERED BY ACTIVITY
Stages 4 & 5 - 12-18 year old players

THEMES & COMPETENCIES
Theme:
+ Team possession with purpose.
+ Group and team defending.
+ Crossing and finishing.

Competencies:
+ Receiving.
+ Passing over short and medium distances.
+ Passing techniques - chip, lofted, driven and swerve.
+ Mobility on and off the ball.
+ Mental conditioning - decision making and speed of play.
+ Support with and without the ball.
+ Pressure, cover and support.

WHY USE IT
Advanced cross-and-finishing activity featuring recycling runs and multiple serves for intensive training.

SET UP
Use 1/3 field and a full-sized goal with a goalkeeper. A flag is placed near the top of the 18 yard box.

HOW TO PLAY
In the base exercise, a group of 5 attackers. A central player serves a ball wide. The flank player dribbles to the end line and crosses. As the wide player dribbles, the finishers fade away around the flag to get out of defenders sight lines and get a better angle to finish. The timing of their runs should coincide with the delivery of the cross. The runners then recycle their runs around the flag and receive a second cross from the other flank. Change positions.

COACHING NOTES
+ Objectives: In addition to technical finishing, timing and location of runs and crosses are critical at advanced levels. Recycling runs create another opportunity after a clearance or long cross.
+ Coaching Tip: Teach the crosser to take his/her last touch toward goal. This touch is the cue for the runners to get into the area at speed.
+ Adaptations: The first serve is an early cross. Vary the cross type (driven or lofted) or location (near post, back post). Add a defender.

+ Central player passes wide and the wide player dribbles to the end line and crosses.
+ 3 attackers run behind the flag (representing a defender) and must time their approach to the goal to arrive when the ball is delivered.

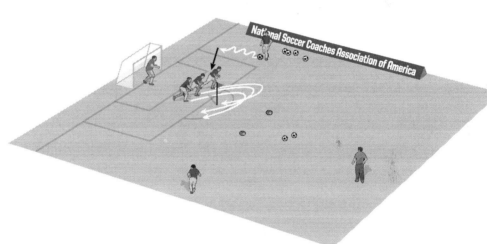

+ Following the first cross the attackers run back around the flag – 'recycle' their runs!
+ A cross is delivered from the other side

+ On the third sequence the wide player drives or lofts in an early cross for the attackers to run onto.
+ The sequence continues with recycling runs and a serve from the other side.

FLANKENSPIEL

STAGES COVERED BY ACTIVITY
Stages 3, 4 & 5 - 9-18 year old players

THEMES & COMPETENCIES
Theme:
+ Group and team defending.
+ Crossing and finishing.

Competencies:
+ Receiving.
+ Passing over medium and long distances.
+ Passing techniques - chip, lofted, driven and swerve.
+ Mobility on and off the ball.
+ Mental conditioning - decision making and speed of play.
+ Support with and without the ball.
+ Defending a cross.

WHY USE IT
Efficient, fun and realistic cross and finish exercise.

SET UP
3rd field, 50 yards wide and 40 yards deep. 2 full-sized goals and a large ball supply. 2 teams of 4-5 and a server for each team in one of their attacking corners.

HOW TO PLAY
A regular game is played, but all restarts initiate a cross. A goalkeeper designated by the coach starts the game – rolling the ball to a teammate. If the ball goes out of play or a foul is committed, the player in the corner crosses the ball. The server from the corner should vary serves and the coach should emphasize the importance of quality runs into the box. Award 1 point for a goal for normal play and 2 points for a goal from a cross. When the goalkeeper gets the ball, it is dead and play starts with a cross. Play to 8 points and then change servers.

COACHING NOTES
+ Objectives: Improve quality of angles and timing of runs and also technical finishing in a pressure game environment.
+ Tip: Discuss with the players the concept of 'framing the goal' – by the players not directly involved in the play moving in line with the goal posts.
+ Adaptations: Move servers up the touch line to initiate early crosses. Add recycling runs by limiting touches to finish and adding a server for each team on the opposite side.

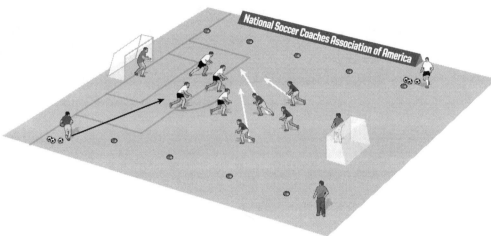

+ Start with a regular game.
+ All restarts initiate a delivery from the corner.
+ Coach determines which team restarts and players must adjust quickly.

+ Bring the crossing position 10-20 yards from the touchline
+ Players must adjust runs and timing accordingly.

+ Add a server for each team on both sides of the field.
+ Central players must recycle runs and prepare for a second cross from the other side of the field
+ Limit finishing to 3 touches.

WIDE ZONES

STAGES COVERED BY ACTIVITY
Stages 3, 4 & 5 - 9-18 year old players

THEMES & COMPETENCIES
Theme:
+ Group and team defending.
+ Crossing and finishing.
+ Team possession with purpose.

Competencies:
+ Receiving.
+ Passing over short, medium and long distances.
+ Passing techniques - chip, lofted, driven and swerve.
+ Mobility on and off the ball.
+ Mental conditioning - decision making and speed of play.
+ Support with and without the ball.
+ Defending a cross.

WHY USE IT
This environment emphasizes wide play and cross-and-finish opportunities and it is easy to progress from no pressure to full pressure.

SET UP
Two equal teams on 2/3 field. Wide players to cross on both sides for both teams in a 10-yard vertical zone. Ball supply in each goal for restarts.

HOW TO PLAY
Play 9v9 in a central zone, 50-60 yards wide and 80 yards long. Goalkeeper starts by serving the ball to his/her team. Normal rules apply, except that a team can only score from a ball crossed from the wide zones. The wide players are uncontested – once a player has a ball the other team cannot challenge. The wide players must deliver crosses into the box from varying angles. Each team focuses on timing and placement of runs to finish their crossing opportunities.

COACHING NOTES
+ Objectives: Early play to wide zones. Good and varied service. Quality runs and finishing.
+ Coaching Tip: Require an increasing number of passes before a pass can be made into the wide zones to simulate more match-like conditions.
+ Adaptations: Players start outside the zones and must play a combination to put a player in the zone. That player is free to dribble and cross.

+ Blues are in possession in the central zone.
+ The player on the ball looks to make a penetrating pass to the wide zone to release a teammate.
+ Wide players cannot be tackled.

+ On receipt of the pass, the wide player dribbles to the end line.
+ Attacking players make runs into the penalty area.

+ As a variation no players are allowed to start in the wide zones.
+ The blue team combine to release a player into a wide zone to cross.
+ A blue player makes an overlapping run to enter the wide zone.

STAGES COVERED BY ACTIVITY
Stages 3, 4 & 5 - 9-18 year old players

THEMES & COMPETENCIES
Theme:
+ Group and team defending.
+ Crossing and finishing.
+ Team possession with purpose.

Competencies:
+ Receiving.
+ Passing over short, medium and long distances.
+ Passing techniques - chip, lofted, driven and swerve.
+ Mobility on and off the ball.
+ Mental conditioning - decision making and speed of play.
+ Support with and without the ball.
+ Defending a cross.

WHY USE IT
Outstanding environment for training box organization, driving attacks to the goal and pressure finishing.

SET UP
18-yard box plus 10 yards (cone line). 2 equal teams of 7 players. A server for each team delivers crosses from the corner with a large ball supply. 4 players in the box and the remaining players line up outside a cone line 10 yards outside the penalty box with soccer balls.

HOW TO PLAY
The goalkeeper starts and restarts play by identifying the server in the corner or a player along the cone line. The servers in the corner play crosses into the box. If the ball is cleared to a player outside the penalty area, they can shoot or play to a teammate in the area. Continue play as long as the ball remains in the area. Goal - 1pt. Great save - 1pt. 3 minutes and rotate.

COACHING NOTES
+ Objectives: Players become more comfortable finishing crosses and shooting opportunities under pressure.
+ Coaching Tip: Its important to clear the 6-yard box at each restart that comes from the cone line so that the goalkeeper has a chance to deal with the shot.
+ Adaptations: Players in the area can lay off a ball for a player on the cone line to finish first-time. Players along the cone line can combine with active players to join the play in the area for the current sequence.

+ Each team starts with a player in the corner ready to serve into the penalty box.
+ Play 4v4 in the penalty box.
+ Additional line of servers 10 yards outside the box.

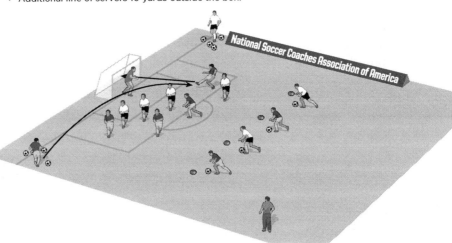

+ A cross from the corner is finished with a first time shot.

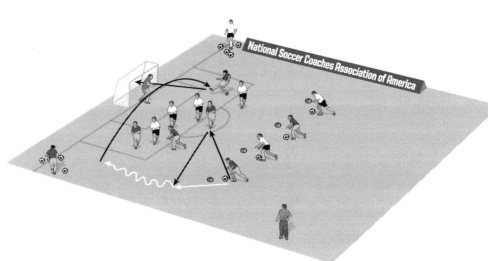

+ The goalkeeper calls the name of a server outside the penalty box.
+ The black server passes to a team mate in the box
+ The server joins the play, dribbles to the end line and crosses for teammate to finish.

10V6 + KEEPER: FRONT THIRD ORGANIZATION

STAGES COVERED BY ACTIVITY
Stages 4 & 5 - 12-18 year old players

THEMES & COMPETENCIES
Theme:
+ Group and team defending.
+ Crossing and finishing.
+ Team possession with purpose.

Competencies:
+ Receiving.
+ Passing over short, medium and long distances.
+ Passing techniques - chip, lofted, driven and swerve.
+ Mobility on and off the ball.
+ Mental conditioning - decision making and speed of play.
+ Support with and without the ball.
+ Defending a cross.

WHY USE IT
Functional training environment - the coach can set patterns and preferences for finishing attacking opportunities.

SET UP
Half field with a full-sized goal and counter goals on the halfway line. Ball supply in all 3 goals for quick restarts. 10v7 (1 Goalkeeper and 6 defenders).

HOW TO PLAY
A scrimmage with the flexibility for the coach to imprint patterns and tendencies for the attacking group. Common topics can include flank and central attacking patterns, organizing the box, getting in behind, changing the point of attack, finishing and more. Allow for coaching team in transition, as the defenders can counter into side goals.

COACHING NOTES
+ Objectives: Can the team read the defense and assess the most promising attack strategy? Is the defense too high (get in behind)? too deep (build up in front - find a seam) or too narrow? Or exposed centrally?
+ Coaching Tip: Allow the players to play for the first few minutes so that they settle into the environment and shape. This period also allows the coach to read and adjust the attackers natural tendencies.
+ Adaptations: Require a particular attacking concept or pattern (i.e. Combine and cross, play through a target player, etc.).

+ 10 attackers (here 4-2-3-1) v 6 defenders (4-1-1) plus a goalkeeper on one-half field with counter goals.
+ Defending team start playing compact.
+ Attacking team find room on the flanks and get the ball wide.

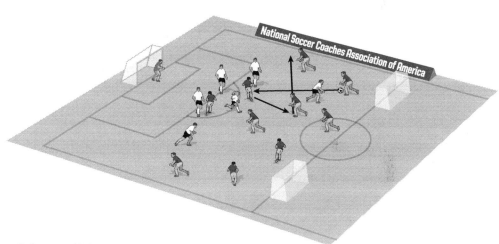

+ Defense too high and tight.
+ Attacking team plays into target.
+ The ball is laid off to set up a penetrating pass up the flank for the wide midfielder to run onto.

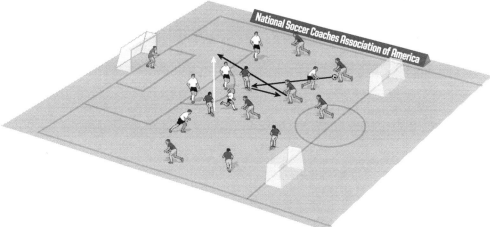

+ Defense too high and not tight.
+ The ball is played to the target who lays it off to the on-rushing midfield player to play in behind.
+ The attacking midfielder has made a blind-side run behind the center back for a pass down the seams.

PRINCIPLES OF PLAY

Principles of play are the underpinning concepts of the game and can be coached from the first stage of development onwards. The principles relate to attacking and defending and should not be confused with systems of play – the formation of the team on the field The principles of play are the same in any system of play. It is important for the coach to know and understand the principles before helping the players to understand. With a good appreciation and excellent technique a team will be able to play any system and style.

ATTACKING PRINCIPLES

There are 5 principles of attack:

1. Penetration
In simplistic terms penetration is the act of breaking through the defense by dribbling, shooting, running or passing. We can start to coach penetration at stage 1 of development.

2. Depth and support
A player in possession of the ball receives help to maintain possession. Support attackers provide forward, backward and sideways options to the attacker in possession. We can start to coach support at stage 2 of development with passing and receiving.

3. Width
The attacking team attempts to stretch the opponent's defensive shape. The attacking players use the width of the field to tempt the defenders from a compact shape covering the dangerous areas in front of goal and in so doing create space. The attackers move the ball to change the point of attack in an effort to find a seam or space between or behind the defense. We can start coaching 'width' in late stage 2 and early stage 3.

4. Mobility
Attackers make runs into different areas of the field in order to draw defenders out of their positions. A coach can commence teaching this principle is best during stage 3 of development.

5. Improvisation, Creativity and Surprise
Attackers will try to break down defenses by employing the element of surprise. Skills such as back-heels, cut backs, flicks, feints and fakes are all used to this end. Comfort on the ball is critical and this training starts in stage 1 of development.

DEFENDING PRINCIPLES

5 principles of defending designed to counteract the effects of the attacking principles:

1. Pressure
Early in the development process a coach should work on individual defending. 1v1 activities are great ways to teach the skill of 'pressure'. The objective of the defender is to force the attacker to make a mistake without over committing to win the ball. The defender must apply pressure to the attacking player with the ball and either win possession, delay the attack by preventing the shot, pass or dribble. 1v1 scenarios can be introduced at stage 1, but formal coaching of pressure commences at stage 2.

2. Cover/Support/Depth in Defense
Following our coaching efforts to teach defenders to apply pressure to the player on the ball, we progress to work with support defenders off the ball. When defending in pairs, the second defender cuts off passing lanes and is ready to revert to the role of the pressure player if the attacker beats the first defender. This principle is ideal to introduce in the stage 2 stage of development once the players have a good handle on the first principle of pressure.

3. Balance
There are a variety of defensive shapes used to counteract an attack. For example, when the ball is central in the midfield area, the defensive shape is more pie shaped with the defender nearest the ball applying pressure and the other defenders retaining defensive balance. A third defender will drop off the ball and get into a position where they can mark a player, follow a penetrating run or step forward to pressure the ball. Naturally, adding a third and fourth defender follows pressure and cover and should be introduced in the third stage of development.

4. Delay/Patience/Discipline/Restraint

All too often young defenders will be over eager to win possession of the ball off an attacker. Impatient defending can result in the loss of defensive shape and compactness. It is important for a coach to teach defenders to read the game and make good decisions on when to win possession, when to apply enough pressure to force an attacker to lose possession and when to force the attack in a direction most beneficial to the team. It is now common place in soccer for coaches to work seriously on transition from defense to attack. Counter attacking and fast breaks are deemed great ways to create an attacking overload as over committed defenders are chasing back to get goal side of the ball. To this end, the defensive principle of delay is paramount. The objective is to slow the attack by forcing the ball to less dangerous areas of the field and allow teammates to get back into position. We can start to work on this principle in the later stage 2.

5. Compactness

Defensive compactness is the polar opposite of Attacking width. The aim is to condense the middle of the field and limit the space and likelihood of penetration. We often see this tactic employed by a less capable team when they are playing against a stronger and more fluent passing team. The phrase 'parking a bus in front of the goal' has been used to describe how difficult it becomes for an attacking team to overcome a compact defense. One can employ this principle in small sided games at stage 3 of development.

SYSTEMS OF PLAY

A system of play is the formation of the team during a game. Commencing post puberty (mid to late teenage years), we can start to focus on 1 or 2 positions in an 11v11 game. However, specializing on one position should not occur until adulthood, and even then the more versatile the player (the ability to perform well in different positions of the field), the more value the player has to the team.

Specific positional training can take many years as each role in the team has a unique set of attributes and demands. It is a mistake to limit a player to one position or role before it is imperative to specialize. To that end, throughout the youth experience, a key role of the coach is to provide players with an opportunity to play in many different roles in the system before they specialize.

As coaches of youth players it is far more important for development that we focus on the principles of play and positioning – and not be over concerned with positions. It takes significant time for young players to understand and execute the principles of play, so patience is extremely important. Repetition and reinforcement is crucial and over time player positioning will improve.

Small Sided Games (Stage 1-2)

If a program insists on playing competitive games with 5 and 6 year old players, a 3v3 format with no goalies is most suitable. Applying a system of play is not appropriate and quite frankly pointless. Naturally, players at this age will likely follow the ball. This is a good sign and coaches should encourage the enthusiasm of young players to participate. The aim is to create as many 1v1 situations as possible with all players attacking and defending.

Small Sided Games (Stage 2)

A 4v4 format and no goalie is appropriate for players 7 and 8 years old, although continuing with 3v3 is also beneficial. Remember, the more players on the field the less touches individual players will get. As the players start to appreciate the basic principles of attack and defense learned in practice sessions, the less frantic the game and the more likely you will observe players working together. The coach can start to introduce a 2-2 formation in the second stage of development. However, the formation the players commence the game in will be quickly lost. Two players in the defensive line and two in the attacking line make straight line passing possible. 2-2 formation promotes the idea of playing in pairs.

A cautionary note; as coaches we want defensive players attacking and attacking players defending, so if an opportunity occurs for a defensive player to collect the ball, penetrate space and create an overload of attackers, we should applaud. Similarly, all 4 players should be coached to get behind the ball and defend when the opponents have the ball.

Small Sided Games (Stage 3)

A 6v6 format – 5v5 on the field with a goal keeper is appropriate for players 9 & 10 years old. 3v3 or 4v4 can also benefit these players. A 3-2 formation is recommended. Although a three line formation with a midfield player is a possible formation, it is not recommended. Adding a third line adds to the complexity of the game and is more difficult for the players at this stage to overcome and certainly harder to coach. The addition of 2 new players including the goalkeeper introduces new tactics and opportunities to work in groups and this is certainly a big enough progression in difficulty. The team formation of 3-2 results in more triangles, a very important tactical concept at this stage of development.

Small Sided Games (Stage 4)

An 8v8 format – 7v7 on the field with a goal keeper is appropriate for players 11, 12, 13 and 14 years old. Smaller playing numbers such as 4v4 and 6v6 will also benefit these players. A 2-3-2 formation is recommended. A midfield line is now introduced as 2 more field players have been added to the team. Several formations are possible, but any formation used must make it easy for the players to execute the principles of play. 2-3-2, produces many triangles and places great focus on transitioning from attack to defense and defense to attack. Many tactics can now be introduced

Full Sided Games (Stage 5)

11v11 format. Choosing to move from one format of the game to the next should not be a question of age, but one of readiness. Many players are not ready to make the transition to 11v11 soccer at age 13 or 14. The tactical and decision making complexities are significant – too much for some players. To this end, don't spend an inordinate amount of time trying to fix 11v11 performance issues in your team practices. Instead, find ways to focus on the developmental needs of the players and continue to reinforce simpler tactics. Remember in the modern game of soccer, defensive players often find themselves with opportunities to attack and score and should thus spend training time working with a balance between defensive and attacking practices. Equally, attacking players should be encouraged to track the opposing defenders as they make their forward runs, so a good appreciation of defensive responsibilities is important.

Summary of Principles and Systems

Regardless of system or style of play, the principles will always remain the same. Successful soccer at all levels determined by one factor - 'technique'. The execution of technique and tactics are highly correlated. Limited technical abilities of the players results in limited tactical opportunities.

As a guide, use the principles of attack and defense as your blueprint for coaching youth soccer. Start with a strong individual technical focus and use the competency matrix to direct you on what is and what is not appropriate. Acquiring the fundamental building blocks of soccer is critical to the development of the player.

Canadian Sports Centers. (2007). Appendix 1 - Physical, Mental and Cognitive, and Emotional Development Characteristics. Retrieved February 20, 2009, from www.canadiansportforlife.ca: http://www.canadiansportforlife.ca/upload/docs/LTAD%20Downloads%20Eng/LTAD_Appendix_1.pdf

Canadian Sports Centers. (2007). Canadian Sports for Life - A Sports Parent Guide. Ottawa, Canada: Canadian Sports Centers.

Department of Health and Human Services - Center for Disease Control and Prevention. (2009). Child Development. Retrieved June 25, 2009, from CDC.gov: http://www.cdc.gov/ncbddd/child/default.htm

Department of Health and Human Services. (2006). Physical Education Curriculum Analysis Tool (CDC). Atlanta: Center for Disease Control.

DiCicco, T. (2009). USA U20 National Team - Post 2008 World Cup Report. Chicago, IL: US Soccer.

National Alliance for Youth Sports. (2008). National Standards for Youth Sport. West Palm Beach, FL: National Alliance for Youth Sports.

Qualifications and Curriculum Authority. (2007). Physical Education - Programme of Study for Key Stage 4. London: Qualifications and Curriculum Authority.

(SPARC), S. a. (2007). Developing Fundamental Movement Skills. Wellington, NZ: SPARC.

Tollison, T. (n.d.). Static v Dynamic Flexibility. Retrieved May 25, 2009, from www.elitesoccerconditioning.com

US Soccer Federation. (2006). Best Practices for Coaching in the United States. Chicago: US Soccer.

US Soccer Federation. Position Statements & Best Practices for Player Development. Chicago: US Soccer.

Made in the USA
Lexington, KY
19 August 2015